HARMONY IS FUN
IN A NUTSHELL

Maureen Cox

All enquiries regarding this paperback edition to:

Mimast Inc
email: mimast@telus.net

From the sale of this book the Author and Publishers will make a donation to The Elizabeth Foundation incorporating The Beethoven Fund For Deaf Children (Charity Registration no. 293835).

Introduction

In response to popular request, Maureen Cox, author of the best selling music series Theory Is Fun, has produced this extended edition of her Harmony is Fun books.

She introduces harmony in a simple way. Scales or keys are families. Chords are family members. Related keys are neighbouring families on the magic circle of keys.

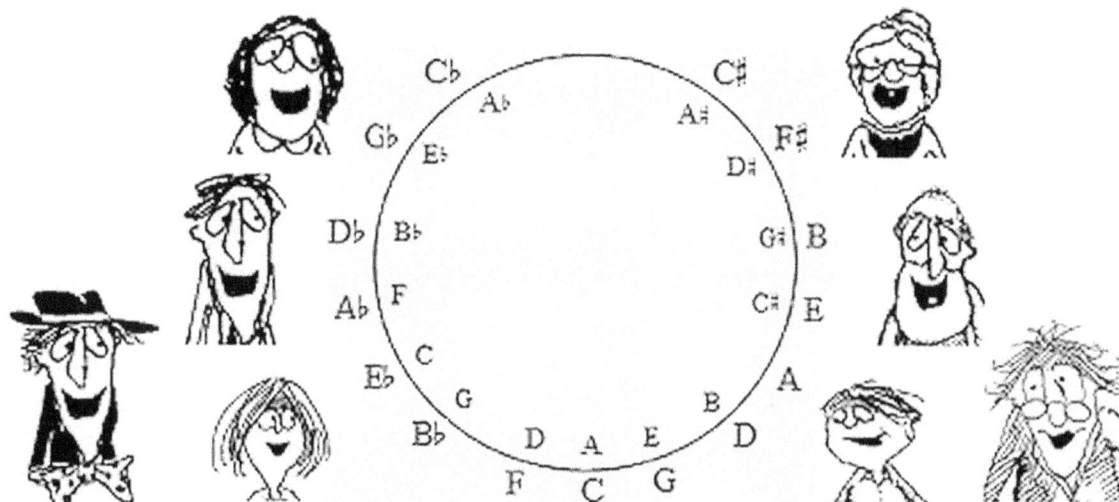

Maureen encourages you to make friends with these families and their members. She also encourages you to listen very carefully to music while you play and sing.

If you want to be able to harmonise a melody, then all you need to do is have fun and follow the easy step-by-step approach in this book.

Acknowledgements

I am grateful to Mimast Inc for inviting me to write this book and thereby giving me the opportunity to convey to others the excitement and enjoyment of harmony.

I should like to thank my professional colleagues and my students, past and present, for sharing my enthusiasm and encouraging this project.

I am grateful to Claire Liddell and Kate Hewson for their helpful input and to Alison Hounsome for her most constructive comments and her excellent Upbeat for Piano series from which I have drawn pieces for harmonisation.

I should also like to thank my husband for his invaluable help in the production and layout of this edition.

Maureen Cox

CONTENTS

SECTION 1

The inner family of Mother, Father and Daughter.

Mother – Tonic chord 1

Father – Dominant chord 5

Daughter – Subdominant chord 4

Begin the magic circle of keys

Notes, keys and fingers

The letters A B C D E F G are the names of the notes in the musical alphabet.

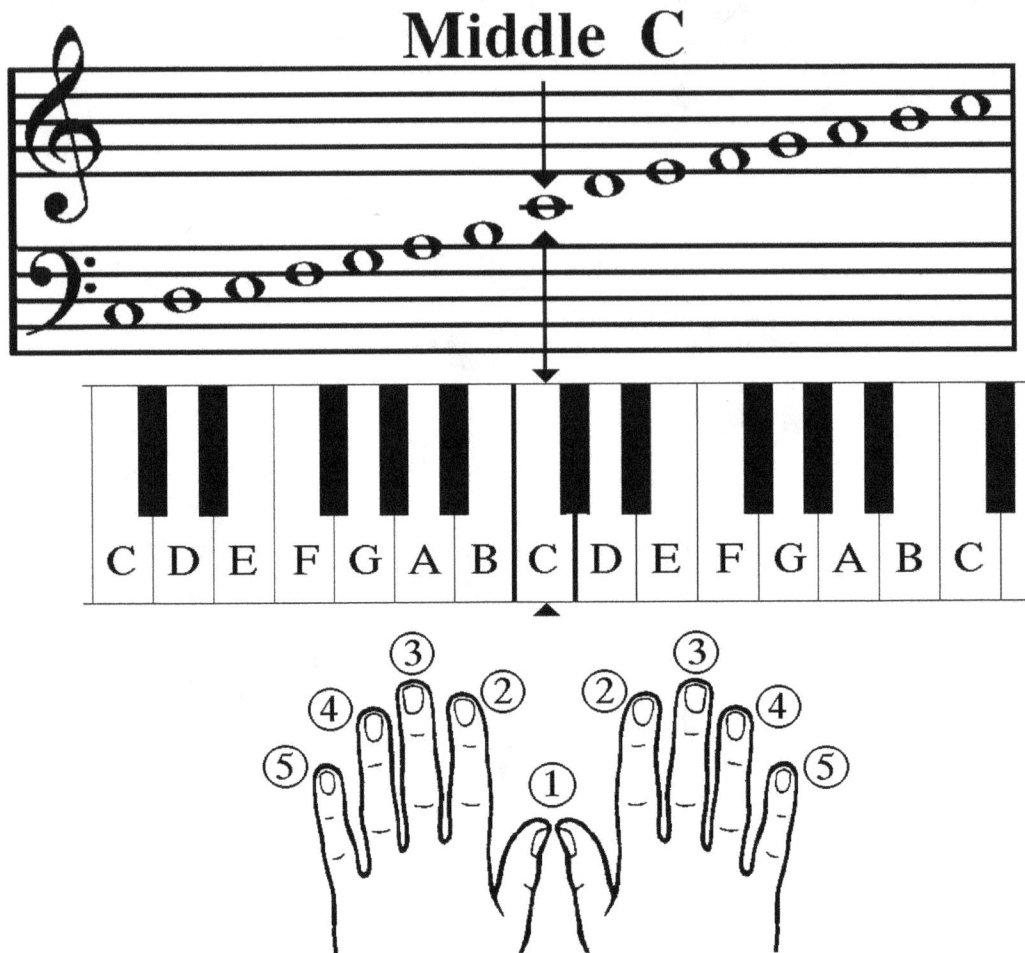

Middle C

C D E F G A B C D E F G A B C

These **numbers in circles** ①②③④⑤ tell you **which fingers** you could use.

Meet the C, F and G Major families

Here are the notes in the **C Major** family.

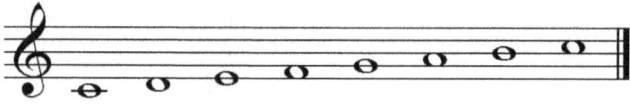

Here is the Mother of the family. Her note is **C**.

She looks after all the notes in the key of **C**.

Mother has a chord. It is built like this.

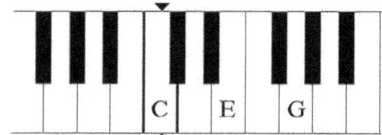

A chord of **three** notes is called a **triad**.

Play Mother's chord with your right hand only.

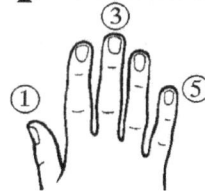

Here again are the notes in the **C Major** Family but this time with the Mother chord.

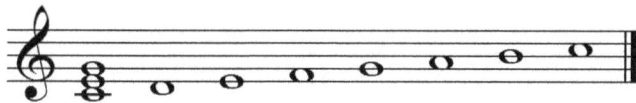

Here is the Father of the **C** Family.

He is a very important member of the family.
What is the letter name of his note? ____

Father has a chord. It is built like this.

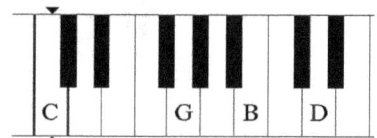

Play Father's chord with your right hand only

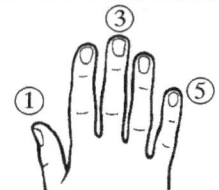

Mother is number 1.
What number is Father? ____

Here are the notes in the **C Major** Family. Can you put in the Mother and Father chords?

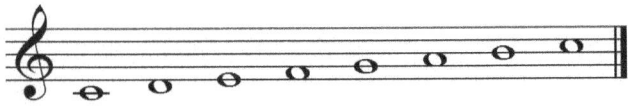

Here is another member of the **C** Family. She is the Daughter.

What is the letter name of her note? ____

Daughter has a chord like this.

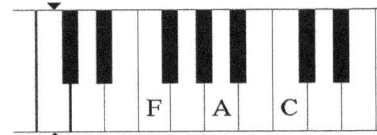

Play Daughter's chord with your right hand only.

Mother and Father are numbers 1 and 5.
What number is Daughter's chord? ____

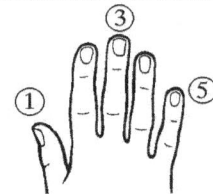

Here is the **Inner Family** in the key of **C**.

Mother is chord 1 because she is built on the first note.
Name her notes. ____ ____ ____

Father is chord 5 because he is built on the fifth note.
Name his notes ____ ____ ____

Daughter is chord 4 because she is built on the fourth note.
Name her notes. ____ ____ ____

Write in the Mother, Father and Daughter chords in the key of **C Major**.

1   4   5

There is a Mother, Father and Daughter chord in every musical family.

Here are the notes in the G Major Family. Write in the Mother, Daughter and Father chords.

Use your right hand to play

Mother's chord →

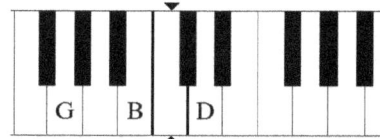

Daughter's chord →

Father's chord →

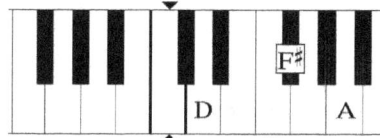

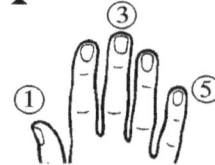

Have fun and write the three chords for the **Inner Family** in the key of **F Major**.

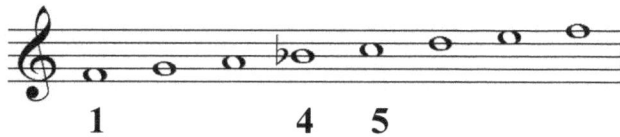

Next-door neighbours

Imagine that the **G** and **F** Families are the next-door neighbours of the **C** Family.

| The **F** Family has one flat (B flat). | The **C** Family has no sharps or flats | The **G** Family has one sharp (F sharp). |

This is the start of the **Magic Circle of Keys**.

Families with flats go to the left

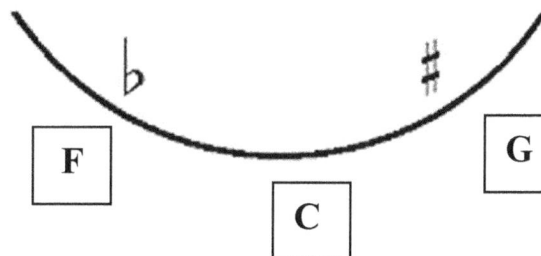

Families with sharps go to the right

You will meet other neighbours later.

Family names

Let us look again at the family of **C**.

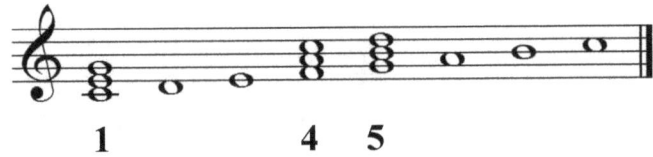

1   4 5

Just as you have more than one name, the **Inner Family members** also have other names.

Mother is **chord 1** and her other name is the **Tonic**.

Father is **chord 5** and his other name is the **Dominant**.

Daughter is **chord 4** and her other name is the **Subdominant**.

Here are three chords for you to draw and then play. Listen to the sounds they make.

Put in the correct key signature.
Draw in the Daughter chord
the **subdominant** chord
in the family of **F Major**.

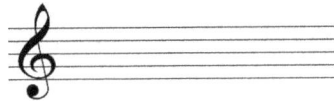

Put in the correct key signature.
Draw in the Mother chord
the **tonic** chord
in the family of **G Major**.

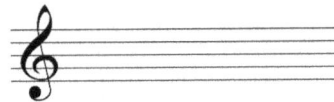

Put in the correct key signature.
Draw in the Father chord
the **dominant** chord
in the family of **G Major**.

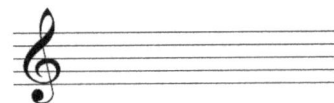

12

SECTION 2

Growing chords

Using the left hand

Harmony with the inner family

Growing chords

You know that the Mother chord in the family of **C** looks like this.

The note **C** is called the **root** because **the chord grows from this note**.

root

The note **E** is the **third** of the chord.

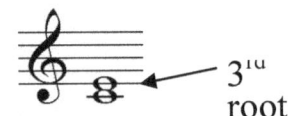

3rd
root

The note **G** is the **fifth** of the chord.

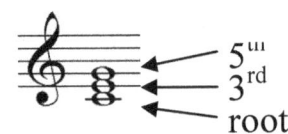

5th
3rd
root

Here is the Mother note in the family of **F**.

Grow Mother's chord by drawing in the other two notes.

1

Grow Father's chord in the family of **C**.

5

Here are two more chords for you to grow.

1

4

Mother chord
in the **C** Family

Daughter chord
in the **G** Family

As you can see, these chords have the same three notes. This often happens in families of keys. However, chord **CEG** in the **C** Family is always Mother and chord **CEG** in the **G** Family is always Daughter.

Mother C and **Daughter G** are *different* people.

Using the left hand

So far you have drawn chords in the treble clef and played them with your right hand. Now you are also going to use the bass clef and your left hand.

Here is **chord 1** of **C Major** for your right hand only.

Here is the same chord with the **root** note **in the bass clef** for your left hand. Play the top two notes with your right hand. Remember ⑤③⑤ are your finger numbers.

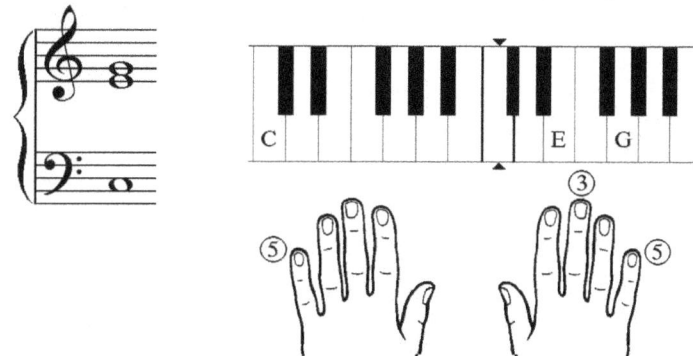

Here are Mother, Daughter and Father chords in the family of **C Major** shared between your two hands. Play and listen to these chords.

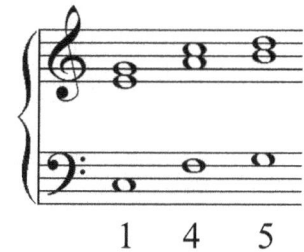

Here are the **root** notes for Mother, Daughter and Father chords in the family of **G Major**. Fill in the notes in the treble clef. Play and listen to the chords.

Fill in the notes in the treble clef for Mother, Daughter and Father chords in the family of **F Major**. Play and listen to these chords.

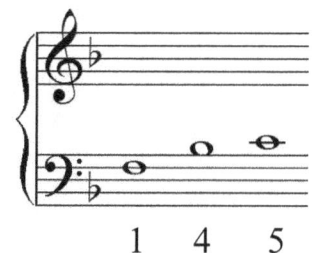

15

A quick look back

Draw Father's chord (5) in the **C** Family.

5

Draw Mother's chord (1) in the **G** Family.

1

Draw Daughter's chord (4) in the **F** family

4

In every musical family, Mother is chord __, Father is chord __ and Daughter is chord __.

In the family of **G Major**, Mother's note is __, Father's note is __ and Daughter's note

is __. Mother's other name is the **t**_____ and Father's other name is the _____.

Daughter's other name is the _____.

The note from which each chord grows is called the **r**_____.

Take care!

Sometimes, a chord within one family has the same notes as a chord within another.

Mother C and **Father F**
are *different* people.

Harmony with the inner family

Here is a tune for you to play. It uses the three chords of the **Inner Family** of the key of **C Major**. Count two beats in each bar.

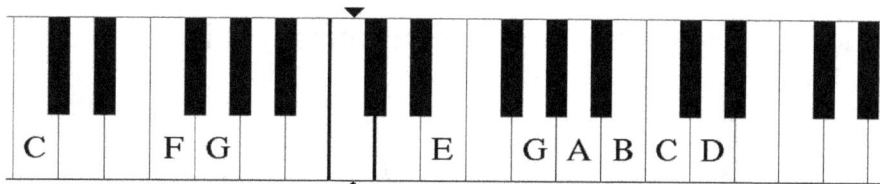

1   5   1   4   1----------

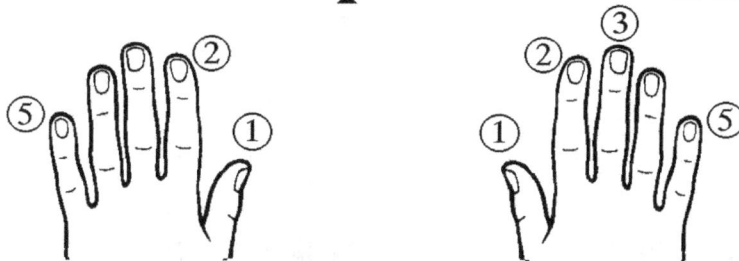

While you play, listen very carefully and notice how the chords fit the melody.

Here are the **Inner Family** chords of the key of **G Major**.

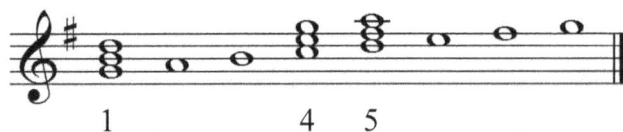

Draw Mother, Father and Daughter chords for this melody. First put the **root** note of each chord **in the bass** clef for your left hand. Now play this piece with both hands.

Draw in the **Inner Family** chords for the key of **F Major**.

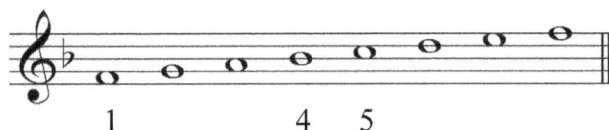

Draw Mother, Father and Daughter chords for this melody. First put the **root** note of each chord **in the bass** clef.

Play the piece with both hands. Count three beats in a bar. Listen carefully to the melody and the harmony

SECTION 3

Closed and open chords

Root and first inversion chords

Block chords

Broken chords

Four-note chords

Notes can change places

You know a chord grows from its **root** and you know the names of the other two notes in a triad - three-note chord.

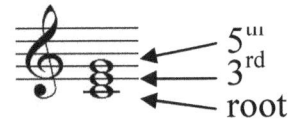

Here are two ways to draw Mother **chord 1** of the **C Major** Family in **root position**. The first is **closed**. The second is **open**, so you may need to play **C** with the left hand.

Now draw Father **chord 5** in **C Major** in two different ways **in root position**. The **root** has been drawn **at the bottom** for you.

Draw Daughter **chord 4** in **C Major** in two different ways **in root position**. Put the **root** note **at the bottom** each time. Play both chords and listen to their sounds.

Root position

Here are the **root position chords** of the **Inner Family** of **C Major** drawn in two different ways. The **root** is **at the bottom**.

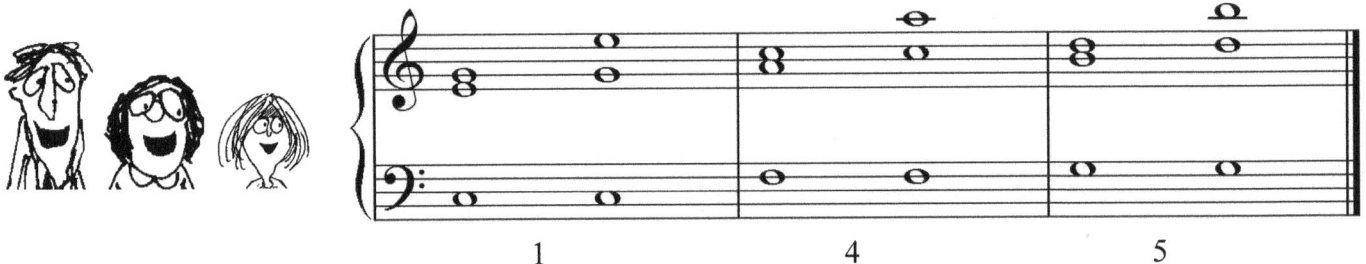

Play the chords with both hands and listen carefully to the different sounds they make.

First Inversion

The **root**, **3rd** and **5th** of a chord keep their names even when the notes change places.

This is Mother **chord 1** in the **C Major** Family in **root position**.

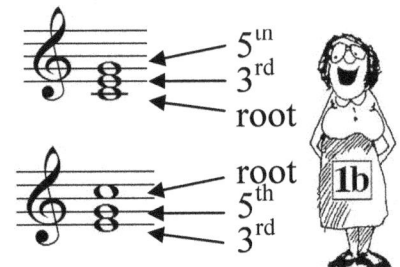

We could draw the same chord with the **root at the top** and the **3rd at the bottom**. This is still Mother chord 1 in **C Major** but we now call it **chord 1b** because the **3rd** is **at the bottom**.

Draw Father **chord 5b** and Daughter **chord 4b** for the **C Major** Family. The **3rd** of each chord has been drawn at the bottom for you.

Play both chords and listen to their sounds.

A first inversion is a chord with the **3rd at the bottom**. Here are three first inversions (**1b**, **4b** and **5b**) shared between the hands. Play these chords. They make different sounds from the chords in root position.

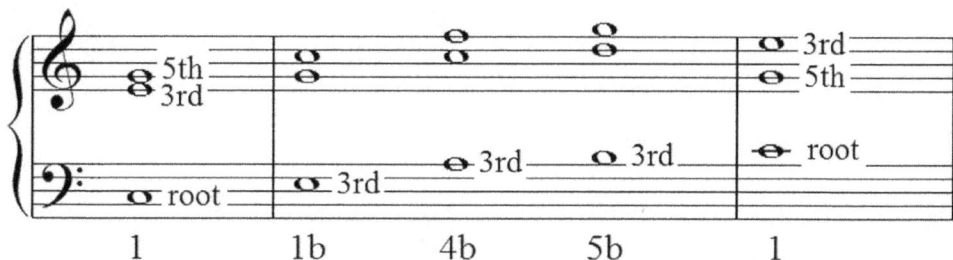

Here are Mother, Father and Daughter chords for the family of **C Major**. They are in **root position** and **first inversion**. Play each chord and listen to the variety of sounds.

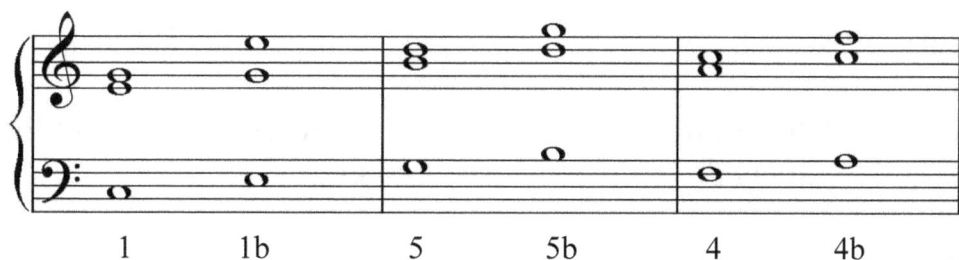

Write Mother, Father and Daughter chords in **root position** and **first inversion** for the family of **G Major**.

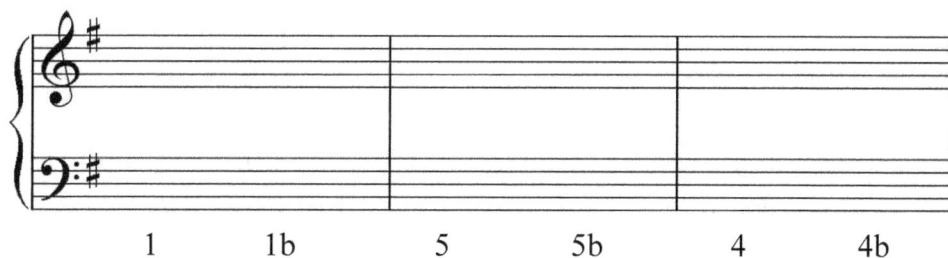

21

Write the chords for the **Inner Family** of F Major in **root position** and **first inversion**.

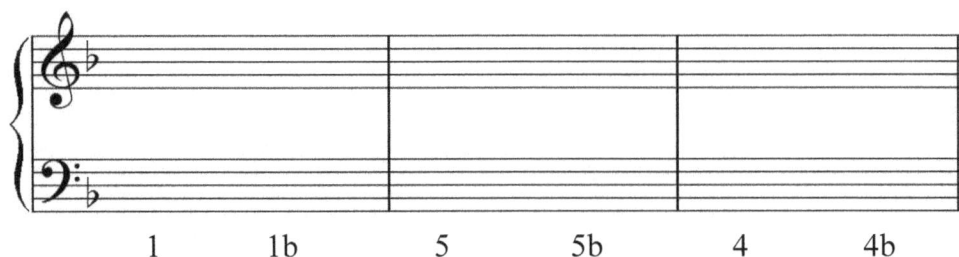

1   1b   5   5b   4   4b

It is important to practise these chords in the key of **C** and in the neighbouring keys of **G** and **F**. This helps you to move more easily between the families. Remember the magic circle of keys.

How many notes in a chord?

A chord is two or more notes played together. Play and listen to these chords.

Here they are with the root in the bass clef.

Notice that we made the *two-note chord into a three-note chord* by **doubling the root**. Play these chords with both hands and listen to their sounds.

Play and listen to these **G** Major tonic chords.

| third doubled *unpleasant sound* | third omitted *hollow sound* |

Now play these *pleasant-sounding tonic chords.*

(a) all three notes with root doubled
(b) 5th omitted and root doubled
(c) all three notes with 5th doubled.

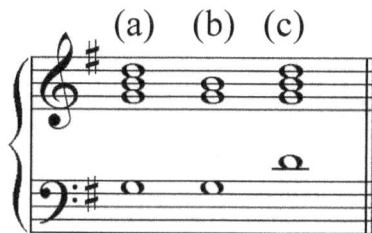

Double the root or fifth of a chord and *never* omit the third.
Do *not* double the third - *yet*!

Harmonising a melody

Here is a melody in the **C Major** Family. Play the melody and listen to it.

Here is the same melody with harmony. Play the harmonised melody and listen to the difference in the sound. Put **r** or **3** or **5** in each empty box to show whether the **root**, **3**rd or **5**th note is at the top of the chord.

5   3   ☐   ☐   r   ☐   ☐   ☐   ☐   ☐

1 ------------ 4   4b   5   5b   1   1b   4   5b   1 -------------

Over to you

Here are eight **C Major** chords.

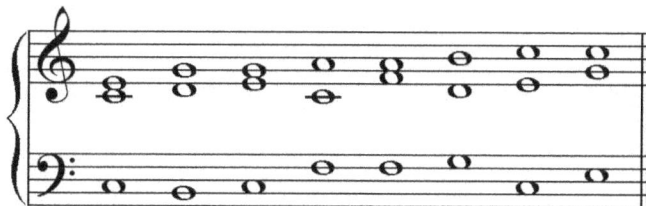

Use the chords to harmonise the melody below using minims and crotchets. The chord numbers are given to help you

1   4   5b   1   1b   4   5   1

23

Broken chords

Play this harmonised melody in the **G Major** Family.

1   5   1 1b 5   5b   1   4   1   5   1

Notice how the **3rd** of a chord gives warmth to the harmony.

warm   cold   cold   warm

You can harmonise two or more melody notes with the same chord. Look at these bars.

1   5   5b

The same melody can be harmonised with the **chords broken up** in the left hand.

Ped.

1   5   1   5   5b   1   4   1   5   1

Pedalling – Try changing the pedal for each new chord.

24

Four-note chords

You can also harmonise the melody with three notes in the right hand and one note in the left.

```
1      5      1     1b  5      5b        1      4    1    5  1
```

After you have played and pedalled this piece, circle in red all the **root** notes of each chord. You will be surprised how many have been **doubled**!

Look ahead

Where do members go in musical families?

Mother goes to Father

Father goes to Mother

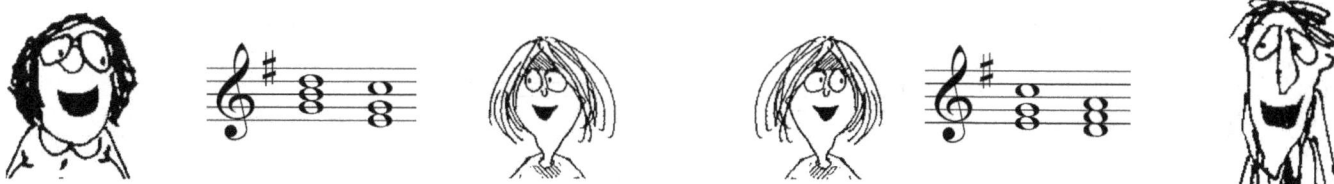

Mother goes to Daughter

Daughter goes to Father

Daughter goes to Mother.

Father chords prefer not to go to Daughter chords!

Fill in the chords for this melody. Use one note for the left hand and two or three notes for the right hand.

Notice in bar 2 that Mother chord is used instead of Father chord for the note **D** because Daughter chord follows in bar 3.

Over to you

Here is a melody in the family of **G** for you to harmonise. The notes for the left hand have been put in. Add one or two notes to the melody for the right hand.

Do not double or omit the 3rd!

Here is the same melody in the **G** Family for you to harmonise. Notice that Mother is often the first chord. This time put some broken chords for the left hand to play.

Practise playing and singing your melody before harmonising it.

Music is flexible

Let's not forget the **F Family**. They live next to the **C Family** on the **Magic Circle**.

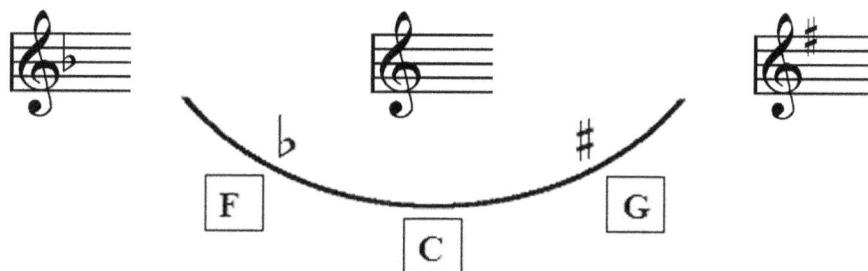

Here is a melody in **F Major** harmonised with **block chords.**

Here is the same melody using **broken chords**.

Use these words to fill the gaps below.

1st	passing	B	Father	C
note	3rd	inversion	D	octave

bar 2: The **5b** means _____ chord in _____ with the ___ note at the bottom.

bar 4: The notes in the left hand make the music move by floating between the _____.

bar 5: Note **G** in the bracket is called a **passing note**. It links note **A** to note **F**.

bar 6: Note __ is a _____ _____ because it links note __ to note __.

SECTION 4

Introducing Father's dominant 7th chord

Resolving

Perfect cadence

Imperfect cadence

Plagal cadence

An extra note

Father chord can sometimes have four notes. This extra note is seven up from the root. The chord is now called the **dominant 7th**.

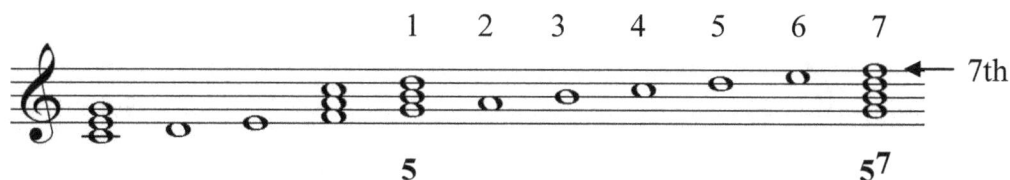

Now there are four

Each **Inner Family** now has **four** chords.

Chord 1	Tonic
Chord 4	Subdominant
Chord 5	Dominant
Chord 5^7	Dominant 7th

Here are all four chords for you to play in each of the **C**, **F** and **G** Major Families.

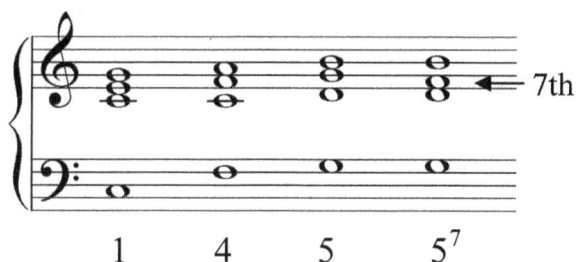

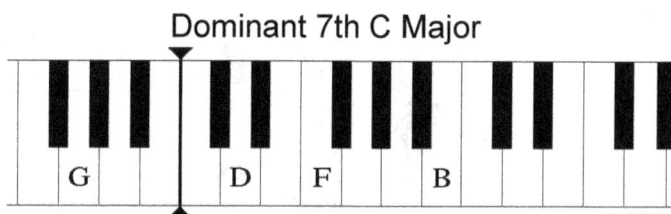

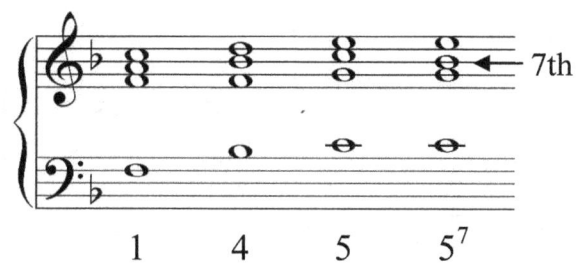

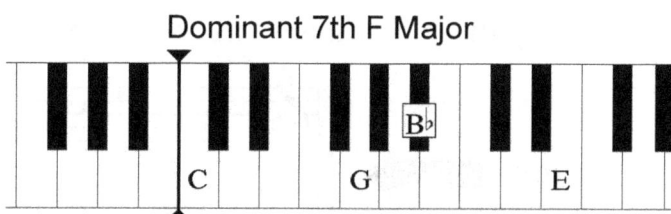

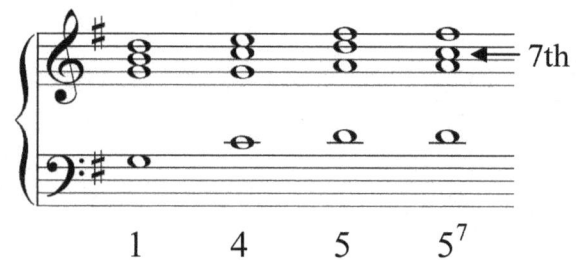

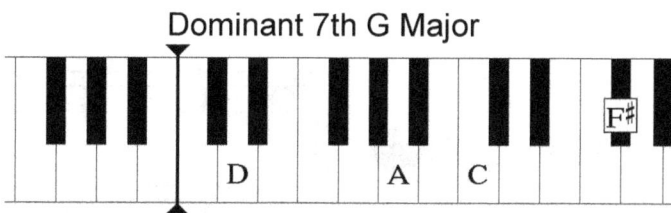

Dominant 7th C Major

Dominant 7th F Major

Dominant 7th G Major

All twelve chords are in root position.

Now there are eight

Each of the **Inner Family** chords can be drawn in **root position** or **first inversion**. Here are the **eight** chords for **C Major**.

Chord 1
Tonic

1   1b

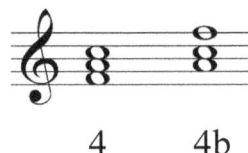
Chord 4
Subdominant

4   4b

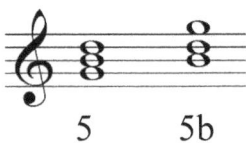
Chord 5
Dominant

5   5b

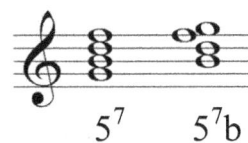
Chord 5^7
Dominant 7th

5^7 5^7b

Resolving

The **7th** note of the dominant Father chord likes to fall onto the note below, as if attracted to it by magic. This is known in music as **resolving**. Here are two examples in the family of **C Major**.

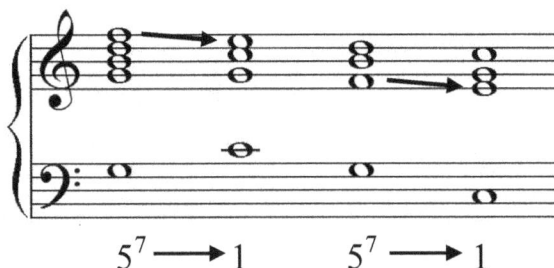

$5^7 \longrightarrow 1$ $5^7 \longrightarrow 1$

Play and enjoy these dominant 7th chords in the musical neighbours of the **C Family**.

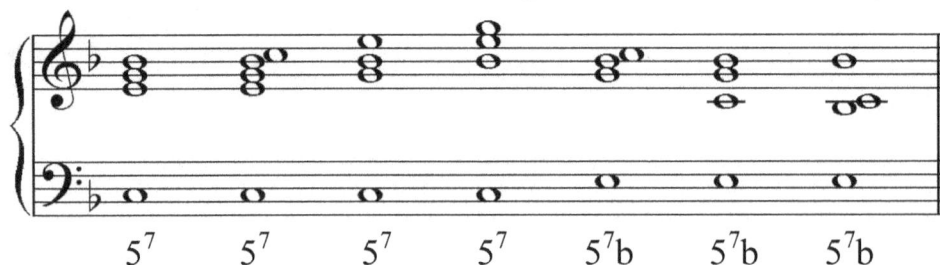

F Major ➡

5^7 5^7 5^7 5^7 5^7b 5^7b 5^7b

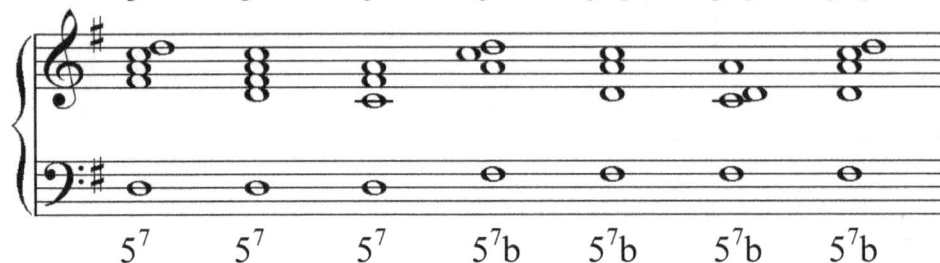

G Major ➡

5^7 5^7 5^7 5^7b 5^7b 5^7b 5^7b

Never double the 7th in a dominant chord.

Here is a mixture of chords for our three musical families. Play them and fill in the empty boxes underneath the chords.

C Major

| | 1b | | 1 | | 5^7b | 1 |

F Major

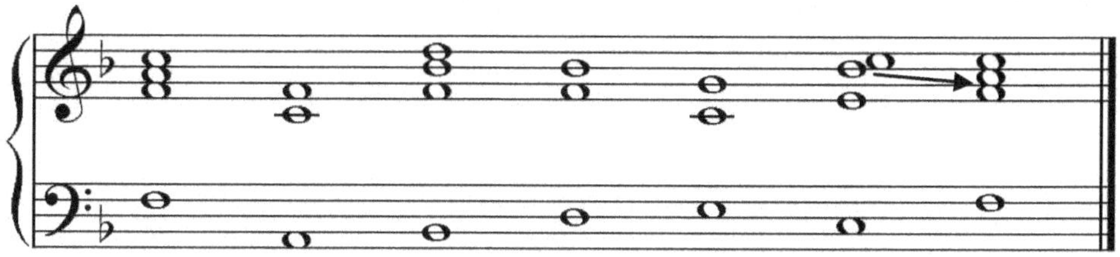

| 1 | | 4 | 4b | | 5^7 | 1 |

G Major

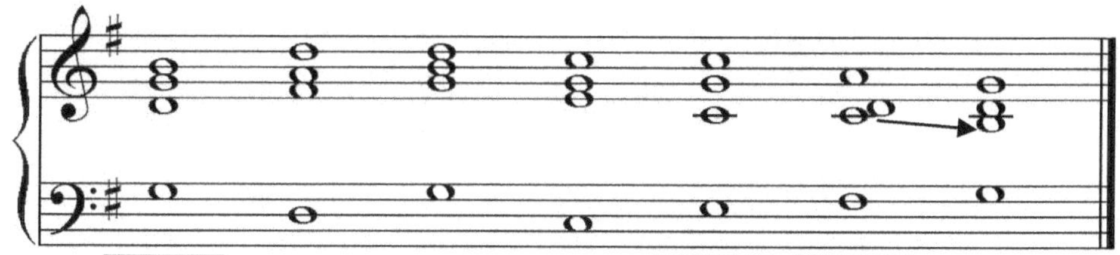

| | 5 | 1 | 4 | | | 1 |

Dominant or dominant 7th?

How do we choose between the Father chord and the dominant 7th chord? The answer is in the sounds they make. Play this example without the extra note.

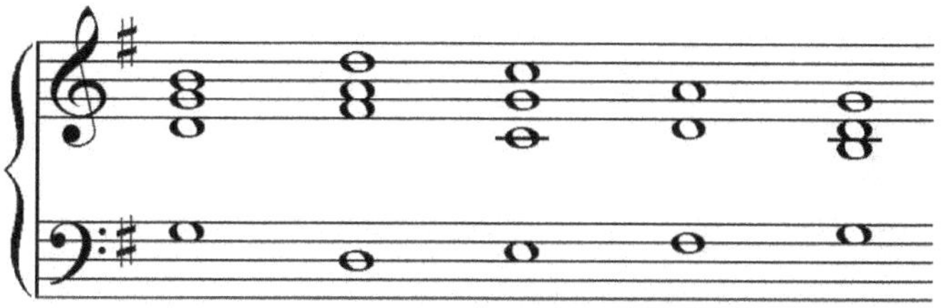

| 1 | 5 | 4b | 5b | 1 |

Now play and listen to the softening effect of the dominant 7th as the note **C** falls like magic onto the note **B** below.

Notice the satisfying **resolving** sound.

1   5   4b   5⁷b   1

In the **C Major Family**, the note **F** has been harmonised by Daughter chord. Until now, she has been the only member of the **Inner Family** with that note. With the arrival of Father's extra note, we have a choice.

chord 4   chord 5⁷

Here are examples of how these chords can be used. In the first example the dominant 7th does **not** appear and the sound is dull.

1   4   1   4   1

In these next two the sound is much richer

1   5⁷   1   4   1

1   4   1   5⁷   1

Complete the five chords in each of these examples and fill in the empty boxes.
Trust your ears to make 'sound' decisions.

| 1 | 4 | 5 | | |

| 1 | 5 | 1b | | |

Cadences

A perfect cadence

When you reach the end of a piece of music you need a very 'final feeling'. For this reason, pieces often end with Father or Dominant 7th chord going to Mother chord. This is called a **perfect cadence**.

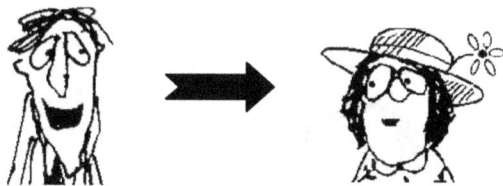

chord 5 to chord 1   **chord 5⁷ to chord 1**

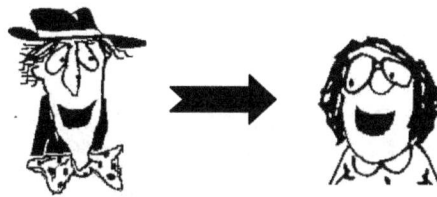

Complete these perfect cadences with Father going home to Mother. Use dominant 7th chords resolving onto tonic chords.

| 1 | 4 | 5 | 5^7 | 1 |

| 1 | 1b | 4 | 5^7 | 1 |

| 1 | 5 | 1 | 4b | 5 | 5^{7}b | 1 |

33

An imperfect cadence

We use this cadence to create an impression of rest at a point where the piece does not end but where a 'breath' is needed. You can think of an **imperfect** cadence like a **comma** and a **perfect** cadence like a **full stop**. For an **imperfect cadence**, Mother or Daughter chord can be used to go to Father chord

chord 1 to chord 5   chord 4 to chord 5

The plagal cadence

Daughter chord going to Mother chord is called a **plagal** cadence. This combination of chords does not give as effective an ending as the perfect cadence. Play and compare these two examples.

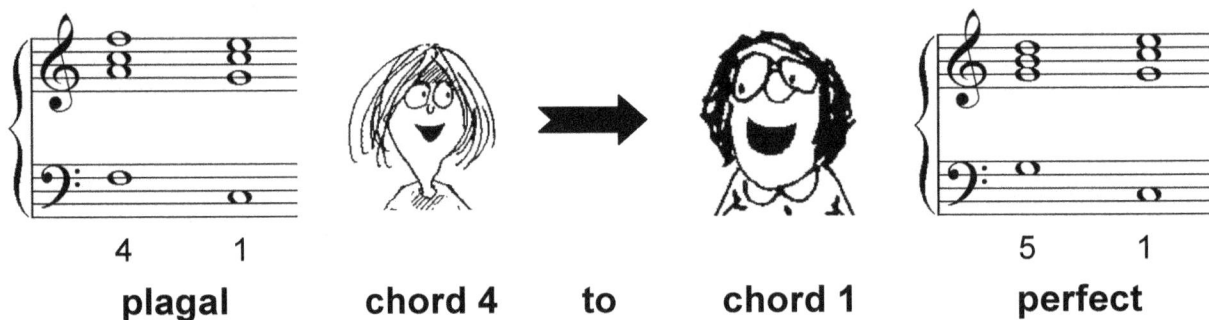

4 1	chord 4 to chord 1	5 1
plagal		**perfect**

Summary

Cadence	First Chord	➡	Second chord
Perfect	Father *dominant*		Mother *tonic*
Imperfect	Mother / Daughter *tonic / subdominant*		Father *dominant*
Plagal	Daughter *subdominant*		Mother *tonic*

SECTION 5

Harmonising melodies

Helpful hints

Three well-known tunes to harmonise

Three harmonised pieces to play

Harmonising melodies

Use each word once only to fill in the gaps.

> Mother   tonic   Father   dominant   Daughter
> subdominant   perfect   imperfect   plagal
> root position   first inversion   root   3rd   5th   7th

A chord with the root at the bottom is in _____. When the third of the chord is at the bottom, the chord is a _____. You can double the _____ or _____ of a chord. You should not double or omit the _____ of a chord. A dominant 7th is a Father chord with an extra note which is the ____ note up from the root. Daughter chords like to go to _____ or _____ chords. Father chords prefer not to go to _____ chords. A dominant chord going to the _____ chord is called a _____ cadence. The _____ chord going to the tonic chord is called a _____ cadence. Chord 1 or 4 going to the _____ chord is called an _____ cadence.

Music is flexible, so remember to mix root position and 1st inversion chords when you harmonise this melody.

1   5   1   1b   4   4b   1   4b   5b   1   1b   4   5   1

Father or Daughter?

Use the dominant 7th or the subdominant to complete the chords in the following melodies. Put the number of the chord you use in the empty box underneath the chord.

Helpful hints

1. Use the magic of Father's dominant 7th resolving onto Mother's tonic chord.

2. Remember Daughter's subdominant chord wants to go to Father or Mother.

3. Use 1st inversions even of Father's dominant 7th chord.

4. Play and sing the melody to find **clues** before you harmonise it.

First melody (four bars)

1   1b   5   5⁷b   1   4   5   ☐ 1 ☐ 5   1

Second melody (four bars)

1 ☐ 1 1b 5 ☐ 1 4 1b ☐ 5   1

37

Third melody (eight bars)

You now know how to use
- Mother's tonic chords
- Daughter's subdominant chords
- Father's dominant chords
- Father's dominant 7th chords

You can decide to write them in
- root position 1 4 5 5^7
- first inversion 1b 4b 5b 5^7b

You can use a combination of
- Block chords
- Broken chords
- Passing notes

You have met resolving and cadences
- Perfect
- Imperfect
- Plagal

You can now harmonise three well-known tunes. Afterwards, you can compare your harmonies with the versions (with words) on pages 42 to 44.

Tune 1

Do you recognise this tune?
Harmonise it by drawing in broken chords
in the left hand.
Two bars have been filled in for you

Tune 2

This tune is about the 10th century saint of Bohemia whose feast day is Sept. 28th. Draw 2 or 3 notes in treble and 1 note in bass.

1 -------- 5b   1 1b 5   4 1b 4 5⁷   1 -------   1b 5⁷b 1   5

1   5   1b   4 1b 4 5⁷   1 -----------   1b -----   4   5

1 1b   5   1b 5⁷b 1   5   1b   4   1

40

Tune 3

This is a Scottish tune which is sung in Scotland on Burns' Night and all over the world at midnight on New Year's Eve

1---------------- 5   5   1 ---------------- 4   4

1b ------ 1   1b   5   5   1b   4   57   1

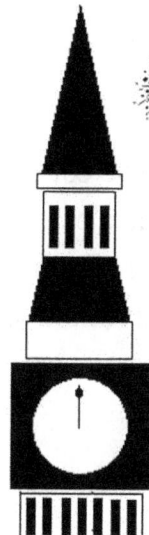

For he's a jolly good fellow

For he's a jolly good fellow,
For he's a jolly good fellow
For he's a jolly good fellow (pause),
And so say all of us

Car c'est un bon camarade,
Car c'est un bon camarade
Car c'est un bon camarade (pause),
Buvons à sa santé

Good King Wenceslas

Good King Wenceslas looked out,
on the Feast of Stephen,
When the snow lay round about,
deep and crisp and even;

Brightly shone the moon that night,
tho' the frost was cruel,
When a poor man came in sight,
gath'ring winter fuel.

"Hither, page, and stand by me,
if thou know'st it, telling,
Yonder peasant, who is he?
Where and what his dwelling?"

"Sire, he lives a good league hence,
underneath the mountain;
Right against the forest fence,
by Saint Agnes' fountain."

"Bring me flesh, and bring me wine,
bring me pine logs hither:
Thou and I shall see him dine,
when we bear them thither. "

Page and monarch, forth they went,
forth they went together;
Through the rude wind's wild lament
and the bitter weather.

"Sire, the night is darker now,
and the wind blows stronger;
Fails my heart, I know not how;
I can go no longer."

"Mark my footsteps, good my page.
Tread thou in them boldly
Thou shalt find the winter's rage
freeze thy blood less coldly."

In his master's steps he trod,
where the snow lay dinted;
Heat was in the very sod
which the saint had printed.

Therefore, Christian men, be sure,
wealth or rank possessing,
Ye who now will bless the poor,
shall yourselves find blessing

Auld Lang Syne

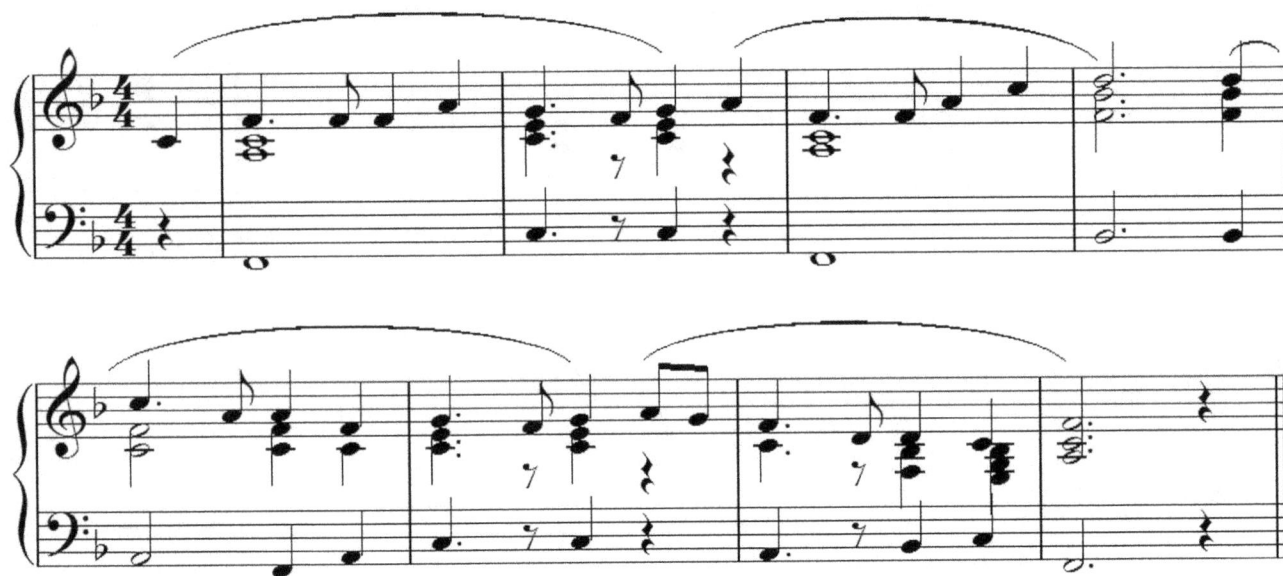

Should auld acquaintance be forgot
And never brought to mind?
Should auld acquaintance be forgot
And auld lang syne?

Robert Burns

SECTION 6

Friends! Romans! Countrymen! Use my numbers!

Expanding the magic circle of keys

Using chords in new keys

Roman numerals I IV V

Second inversion chords

More neighbours

In Section 1 on page 9 you met three families. This began the **Magic Circle of Keys.**

The **F** Family has one flat (B flat).	The **C** Family has no sharps or flats	The **G** Family has one sharp (F sharp).

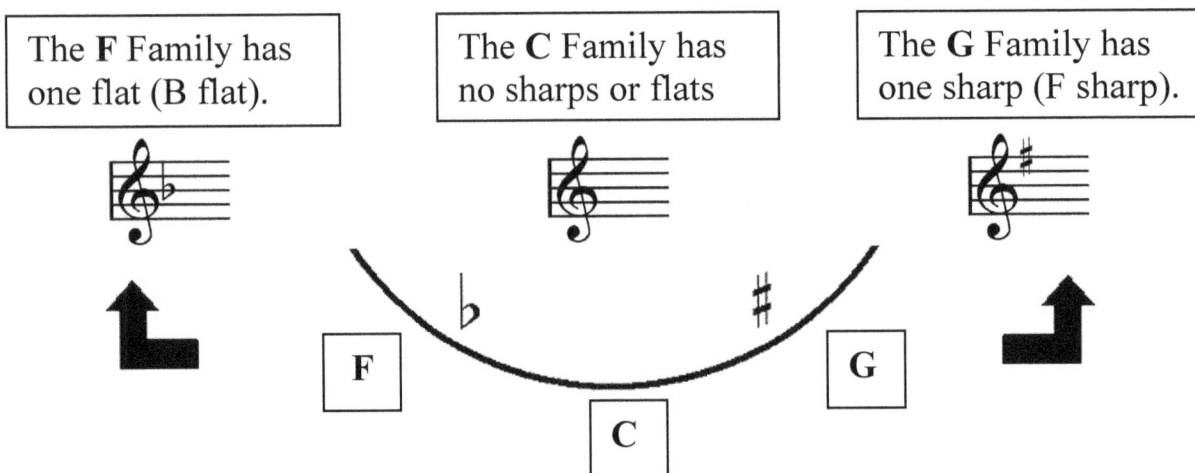

You will now meet some more neighbours so that you can expand the magic circle of keys and increase your harmonising abilities.

D Major Family has 2 sharps: F# and C#

A Major Family has 3 sharps: F♯ , C♯ and G♯

B♭ Major Family has 2 flats: B♭ and E♭

E♭ Major Family has 3 flats: B♭ E♭ and A♭

The **Magic Circle of Keys** has grown.

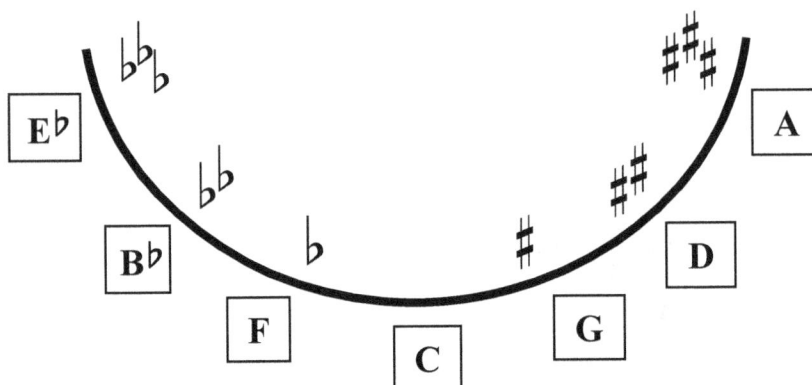

The inner family with new keys

Here are the notes in the **D Major** Family with the Mother, Daughter and Father chords.

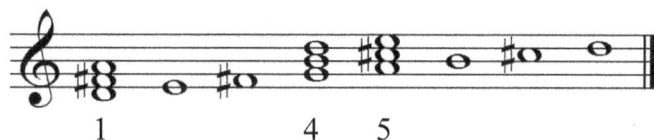

Use your right hand to play

Mother's chord

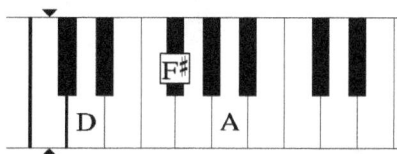

Father's chord

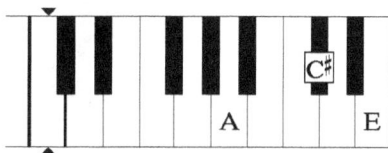

Daughter's chord

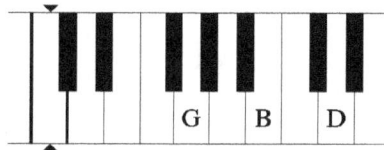

Now repeat the exercise for the **E♭ Major** Family. Remember there are three flats.

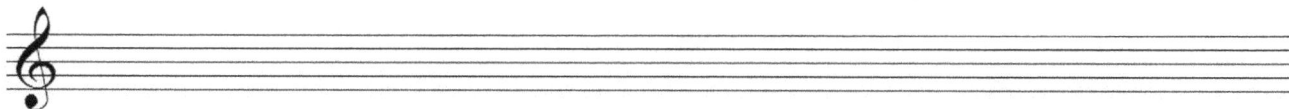

Play each chord with your right hand and listen to their sounds.

Getting to Know the New Keys

Play each chord after you have drawn it.

Draw **with** key signatures:

Mother's chord in the **A Major** Family

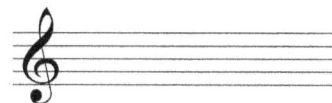

Father's chord in the **E♭ Major** Family

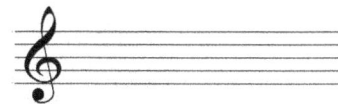

Daughter's chord in the **B♭ Major** Family

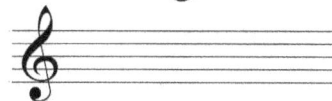

Father's chord in the **D Major** Family

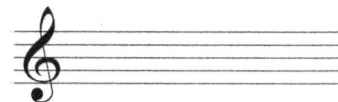

Daughter's chord in the **E♭ Major** Family

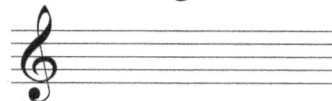

47

Remember the sharps and flats

Draw **without** key signatures but put in any necessary sharps or flats:

Mother's Chord [the Tonic] in **D Major**

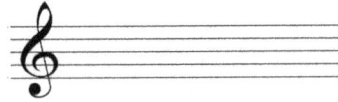

Daughter's chord [the Subdominant] in **E♭ Major**

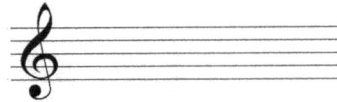

Father's chord [the Dominant] in **A Major**

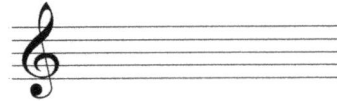

Daughter's chord [the Subdominant] in **B♭ Major**

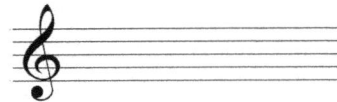

Play each chord. Does it sound right? Check for those sharps and flats.

Key signatures in the bass clef

It is important to be absolutely sure of your key signatures. That means knowing where to place sharps or flats in the bass clef as well as in the treble clef.

Write these key signatures in the bass clef:

D Major

B♭ Major

A Major

E♭ Major

Look at page 46 to check your answers.

Using treble and bass clefs

Here are Mother, Daughter and Father chords in the **D Major** Family. Using both hands, play and listen to these chords.

1   4   5

1   4   5

Here are the **root** notes for Mother, Daughter and Father chords in the **E♭ Major** Family. Add the notes in the treble clef. Play and listen to these chords.

Fill in the notes in the treble clef for the Mother, Daughter and Father chords in the **A Major** Family. Play and listen to these chords.

1   4   5

Harmony with the inner family

Here is a tune for you to play and enjoy. It has the three chords of the **Inner family** of **D Major**. Remember to play the **sharps.**

1   4   1   5   1

Here is a similar tune in **E♭ Major**. Don't forget to play the **flats.**

1   4   1   5   1

49

Roman numerals

So far we have been writing 1, 4 and 5 for Mother [Tonic], Daughter [Subdominant] and Father [Dominant] chords. **Roman Numerals I, IV** and **V** are usually written.

 I    IV   V

Let's get used to them now. Draw in the **Inner Family** chords for

E♭ Major
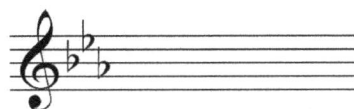
I   IV   V

A Major.
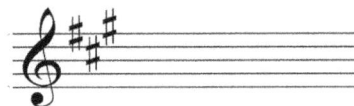
I   IV   V

Harmonise these melodies

Draw the chords for each of these melodies putting the **root** note **in the bass** clef for your **left** hand. Play each piece, counting carefully. Listen to the melody and harmony.

A tune in **E♭ Major**

I ------------   V -----------   I -------------   IV   V   I

A tune in **A Major**

I -----------------   IV -----   I   IV ------   V ------   I

50

Father's dominant 7th chord

So far we have used the Inner Family chords without the Dominant 7th of our new neighbours. Here are Father's two chords in D Major.

Draw the dominant and dominant 7th chords in other new keys:

E♭ Major   A Major   B♭ Major

V   V7   V   V7   V   V7

Play each pair of chords and listen to their different sounds.

Root position

In Section 3 on page 20 you learnt to draw root position chords in two different ways. Draw the closed and open chords for the Inner Families of D Major and E♭ Major. All the roots and two tonic chords have been drawn for you.

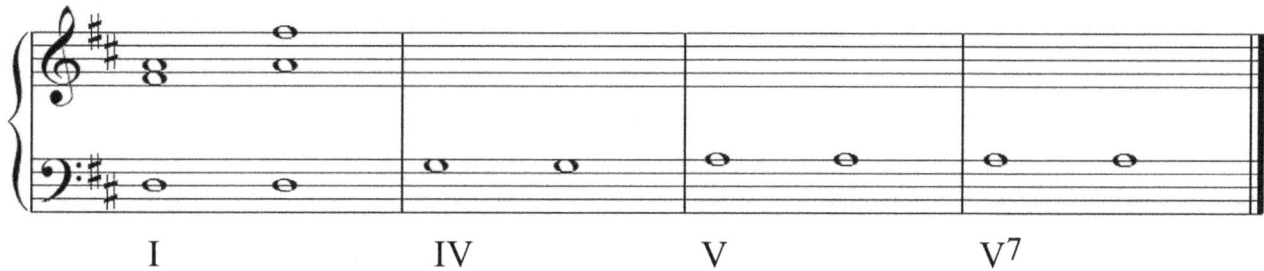

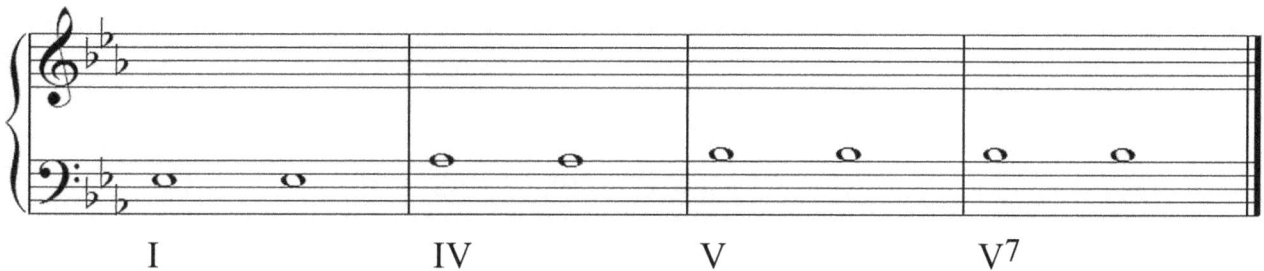

I   IV   V   V7

I   IV   V   V7

For the open V7 chords, you may need to play two of the notes with your left hand.

51

First inversion

You learnt in Section 3 on page 20 that a **first inversion** chord has the **3rd at the bottom**. Here is Mother chord in **A Major** in **root position** and in **first inversion**.

☀ b means the **3rd at the bottom of the chord**

1   1b

Draw Daughter chord in **E♭ Major** in **root position** and in **first inversion**.

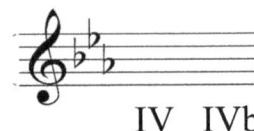

IV   IVb

Now draw the **Dominant 7th** chord for Father in **B♭ Major** in **root position** and in **first inversion**. Remember Father's extra note.

V   V⁷b

Play each chord and listen to the sound.

Second inversion

A **second inversion** has the **5th at the bottom** and a letter **c** with the chord number.
Here is Mother chord in **C Major** drawn in

    root position [I]

        first inversion [Ib]

            second inversion [Ic]

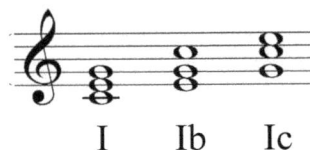

I   Ib   Ic

☀ c means the **5th at the bottom of the chord**

Play the following chords.

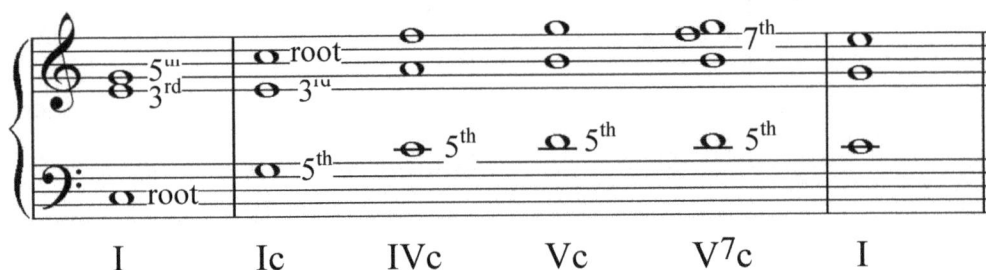

I   Ic   IVc   Vc   V⁷c   I

☀ In any chord, the **order of notes above** the **bottom note** can often be changed.

52

A quick look back

The D Family has ____ sharps. Its next-door-neighbour ___ **Major** has 3 ____. The ___

Major Family has 2 flats. Its next-door neighbour ___ **Major** has ____ flats.

In every musical family _____ chord is the tonic with the Roman numeral I.

Daughter chord is the _____ with the Roman numeral ____. Father chord is the

_____ with the Roman numeral ____. Father chord can have an extra note, seven

up from the root: his chord is then called the _____ 7th.

Fill in the gaps with help from the letters and words in the box.

> c   second   b   inversion   3rd

A first inversion chord has the ____ note of the chord at the bottom. A _____

inversion chord has the 5th at the bottom. First inversion chords have the letter ___ after

the Roman numeral. Chords followed by the letter ___ are known as second _____

chords.

Take care!

Sometimes, a chord within one family has the same notes as a chord within another.

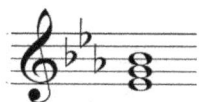

Mother E♭ and Daughter B♭ are *different* people.

Always look at the key signature to identify the family.

Here are the **Bb Major** Family chords in **root position**, **first inversion** and **second inversion**. Notice that the **root**, **3rd** or **5th** is at the bottom of the chord. Play the chords.

I   Ib   Ic   IV   IVb   IVc   V   Vb   Vc   V7c

Now draw these chords for the of **Eb Major**. Father's **dominant 7th** chord and the bottom notes, **root**, **3rd** or **5th**, have been drawn for you. Play all these chords.

I   Ib   Ic   IV   IVb   IVc   V   Vb   Vc   V7c

Draw these chords for the **Family** of **G Major** in **root position**, **first inversion** and **second inversion**. The bottom notes, **root**, **3rd** or **5th**, have been drawn for you.

I   Ib   Ic   IV   IVb   IVc   V   Vb   Vc   V7c

Now draw these chords for the **Family** of **A Major** and play them.

I   Ib   Ic   IV   IVb   IVc   V   Vb   Vc   V7c

Practise these chords in all keys. This will help you to move easily between musical families in the magic circle of keys.

54

Harmonising a melody

Here are melody notes from the **tonic**, **dominant**, **subdominant** and **dominant 7th** chords in four Major keys. Draw in the missing notes, shared between the two hands, to complete the harmonies.

D Major

I   Ib   Ic

Eb Major

V   Vb   Vc

Bb Major

IV   IVb   IVc

F Major

V^7 V^7b V^7c

Play all the chords and listen to the sounds.

Here is a melody in the key of **Eb Major.** Play the melody and listen to it.

Here is the same melody with harmony. Put the **missing chord names** in the six boxes.

I   IV   [   ] Ib [   ]   [   ] Ib [   ] IV [   ] Ic [   ] I

Now play the harmonised melody and listen to the difference in the sound.

55

Over to you

Here are chords in the key of **B♭ Major**. Put their names in the empty boxes.

Use the chords to harmonise the melody below using minims and crotchets. The chord numbers are given to help you. Play your harmonised melody.

I   IVc   V⁷b   I   Vb   Ib   IVb   Ic   V⁷   I

Here are all the melody notes from the chords you have met so far in the **C Major** and **D Major** Families. Fill in the missing notes, shared between the two hands, to complete the harmonies. Play your chords.

I   Ib   Ic   IV   IVb   IVc   V   Vb   Vc   V⁷c

I   Ib   Ic   IV   IVb   IVc   V   Vb   Vc   V⁷c

Now that you can draw **root position**, **first inversion** and **second inversion** chords for familiar keys, you are ready to meet a new set of related families.

56

SECTION 7

The magic circle grows - Minor relatives

Visitors

Cousin – supertonic – chord II

Grandfather – mediant – chord III

Grandmother – submediant – chord VI

Minor relatives

Each Major Family is related to a Minor Family.

For example, **C Major** and **A Minor** are related. Count **down three semitones** from **C** on the keyboard and you reach **A**.

C Major and **A Minor** have the same key signature - **no sharps or flats**.

Discover more relatives

What is the **Relative Minor** of **G Major**?

D Major is related to **B Minor**

Count three semitones to find the missing relatives.

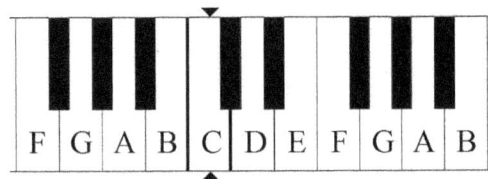

Fill in these key signatures in both clefs.

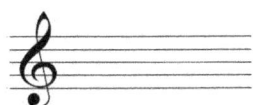

B♭ Major is related to _____ **Minor**

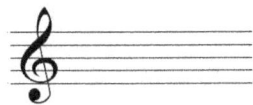

A Major is related to _____ **Minor**

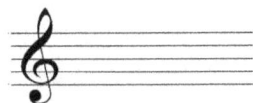

F Major is related to _____ **Minor**

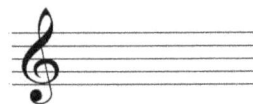

E♭ Major is related to _____ **Minor**

With the Minor Families, you have the key to unlock a whole new world of harmony.

The magic circle grows

Major Families are on the **outside** of the circle and have the same key signatures as their Minor relatives on the **inside** of the circle.

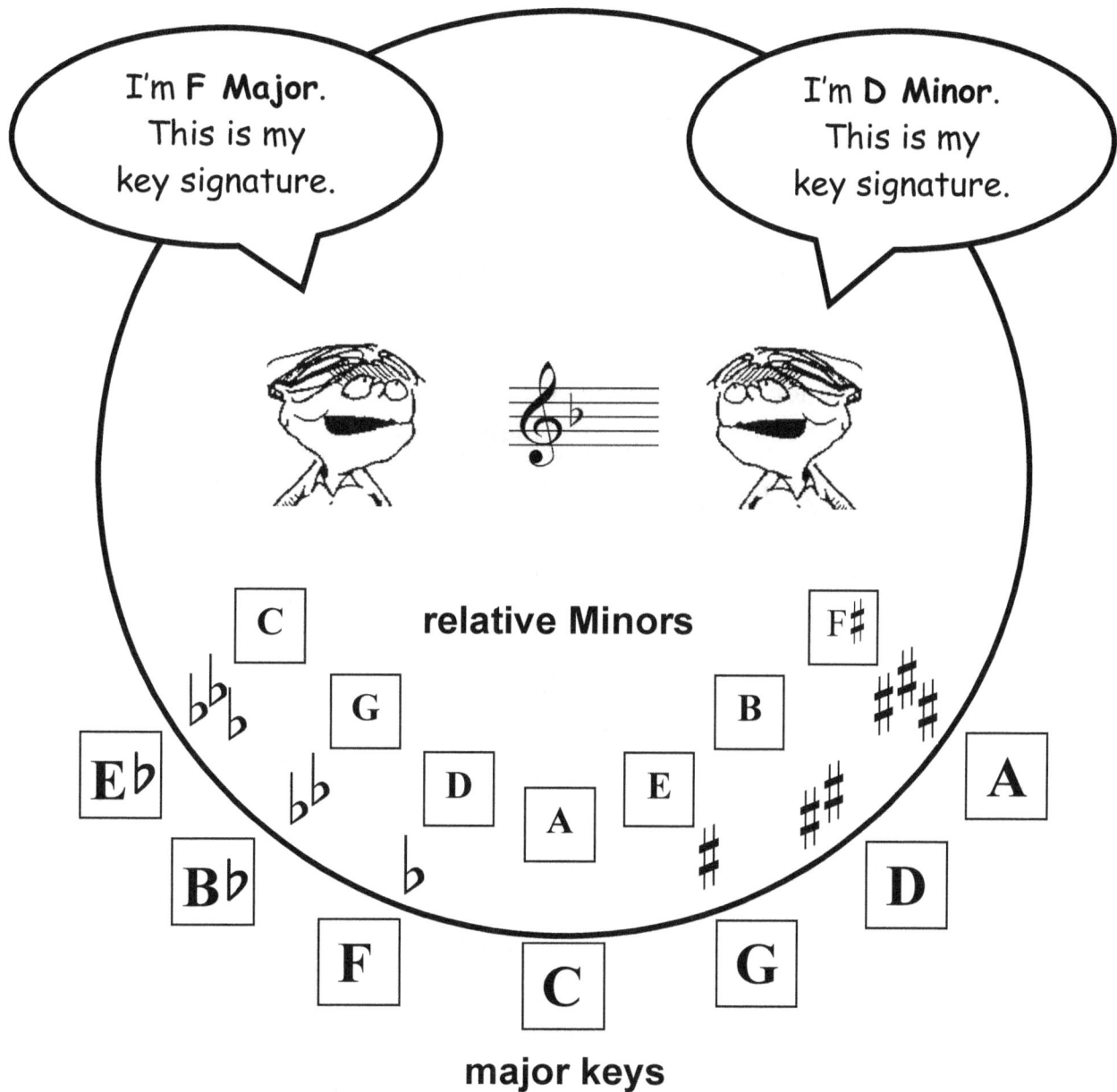

You will find the complete circle of keys in Section 13 at the end of this book.

Minor differences

To understand the differences between Major and Minor Families you have to look at all their notes. Here is the scale of **C Major** going up ↑ then down ↓.

Here is the scale of **A Harmonic Minor**. The **7th** note has been raised by one semitone ascending ↑ and descending ↓.

Play the two scales and listen as you play. Harmonies and tunes in a Minor key may sound sadder than those in a Major key.

There are two forms of Minor scale. In this section you meet the **Harmonic** form. You will meet the **Melodic** form in Section 10. All major and minor scales are in section 13,

Drawing Minor family chords

Draw these **root position** chords for the **Family** of **D Minor**. Remember to raise the 7th note in Minors: see ☺ below.

E Minor		D Minor
 I		 I
 IV		 IV
 V ☺		 V
 V7 ☺		 V7

A visit from Cousin: supertonic – chord II

In each family **Daughter** has a **Cousin** who can sometimes take her place when you are writing your harmonies.

Look at the chords for all the notes of the **C Major Family**.

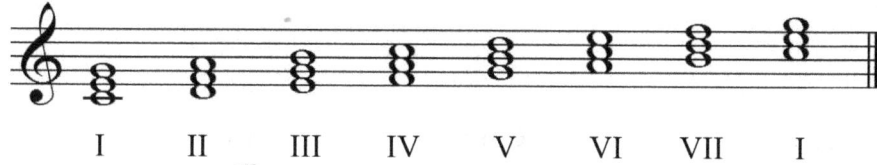

Look at **Daughter** chord.

Chord IV has **F** at the bottom and the notes are the same as the **Tonic** chord of **F Major**.

What is the **relative Minor** of F Major? __

minor   major

Look again at the **C Major Family** chords.

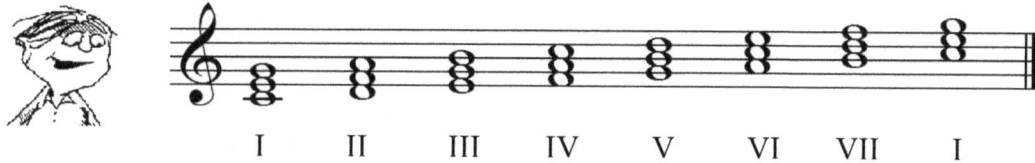

Which chord in **C Major** has the same notes as the **Tonic** chord of **D Minor**? ___

Cousin is the **Supertonic - chord II**.

When harmonising a melody you can sometimes use Cousin **chord II** in place of Daughter **chord IV**. Cousin can be a welcome visitor in any musical family.

Chord I	Tonic
Chord II	Supertonic
Chord IV	Subdominant
Chord V	Dominant
Chord V^7	Dominant 7th

Play this tune in **A Major**.

Now play it again and hear how Cousin replaces Daughter in bar 2.

Now play these versions in **B♭ Major**. Where are the Cousin and Daughter chords?
Put **IIb** and **IV** in the correct boxes.

62

Meet Grandfather: mediant – chord III

In each musical family **Grandfather** may visit and take the place of **Father**.

Here are the chords for all the notes of the **C Major Family**. Look at **Father** chord **V**.

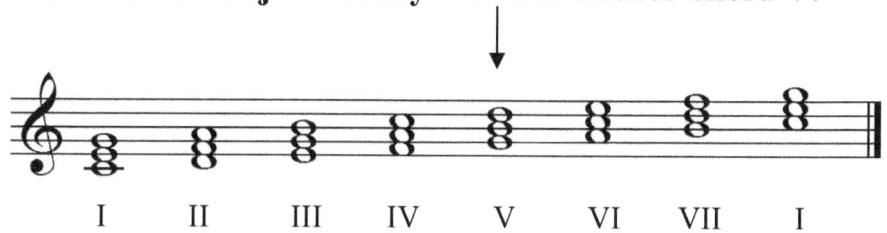

I   II   III   IV   V   VI   VII   I

Chord **V** has **G** at the bottom and the same notes as the **Tonic** chord of **G Major**.
What is the **relative Minor** of G Major? __

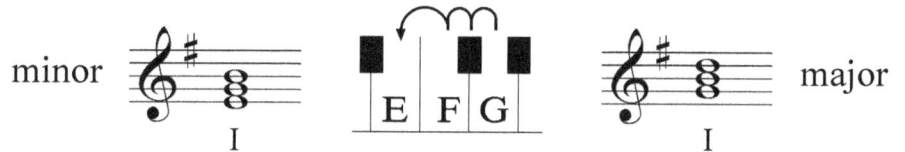

minor   I   E | F | G   I   major

Look again at the chords in the **C Major Family**. Which chord has the same notes as the
Tonic chord of **E Minor**? ___

Grandfather is the **mediant** - chord **III**.

Grandfather **chord III** can sometimes replace Father **chord V** when harmonising a
melody.

Chord I   Tonic
Chord II   Supertonic

**What about me?
Isn't there someone
who can give me a rest?**

**Soon, very soon, but let's
first learn to use
Grandfather's chord.**

Chord III   **Mediant**
Chord IV   Subdominant

Chord V   **Dominant**
Chord V^7 Dominant 7th

Play this tune in **A Major**.

I V＿＿ I IVb Ic [V＿＿V⁷] I

Now play this version and hear how Grandfather replaces Father in bar 1.

I III＿ I IVb Ic [V＿V⁷] I

Play these two versions of a tune in **B♭ Major**. Put **V** and **III** in the correct boxes.

version 1

I [   ] I IVb＿ Ic [V＿V⁷] I

version 2

I [   ] I IVb＿ Ic [V＿V⁷] I

64

Grandmother arrives: submediant – chord VI

There is help at last for Mother. Her replacement is **Grandmother**.

You can discover **Grandmother** chord in exactly the same way as you discovered Cousin and Grandfather chords. Look at **Mother** chord in the **C Major Family**.

I   II   III   IV   V   VI   VII   I

Chord **I** is the **Tonic** with **C** at the bottom.
What is the **relative Minor** of C Major? __

minor   major

Which chord in **C Major** has the same notes as the **Tonic** chord of **A Minor**? ___

☀ **Grandmother** is the **submediant** - chord **VI** *

Play these two versions of the same tune to hear how Grandmother can replace Mother.

I   V___   I   IVb__   Ic   [V__V⁷]   I

I   V___   VI   IVb__   Ic   [V__V⁷]   I

* The submediant is sometimes called the superdominant

65

Now play the complete piece in **A Major** using chords from the **Inner Family** only.

 I    IV    V    V⁷

I   Vc__   Ib   IV__   Ic   Vb__   I   Vb

I   V____   I   IVb   Ic   [V__V⁷]   I

This version in **B♭ Major** uses the chords of our three visitors. Play it and then write **IIb**, **III** and **VI** in the correct boxes.

I   Vc__   Ib   [ ]   Ic   Vb   I   Vb

II

III

VI

I   [ ]   [ ]   IVb   Ic   [V__V⁷]   I

66

SECTION 8

Resolving and cadences revisited

Block chords

Broken chords

Pedalling

Practice to improve your harmonising skills

Resolving

In Section 4 on page 30 you learnt that the **7th** note of the dominant Father chord likes to fall onto the note below. This gives a magical effect when **chord V^7** or **V^{7}b** resolves to **chord I** in a **perfect cadence**. Play and listen carefully to these two perfect cadences.

V → I

V^7 → I

You also learnt in Section 3 that chords may be **closed** or **open**. Play these two perfect cadences in **A Major** and listen to the difference. Circle the 7th note in each chord.

V^{7}b → I

V^{7}b → I

Remember the rule - we should **never double the 7th** in a **dominant chord**.

A perfect cadence is like a 'full stop' and an **imperfect cadence** is like a 'comma' in music. Play these two imperfect cadences.

I → V

IV → V

Play the following cadences. Put the chord number in each box and write imperfect or perfect for the name of each cadence.

D Major   A Major   B♭ Major   E♭ Major

_____   _____   _____   _____

68

Block chords, broken chords and pedalling

Play this piece in **G Major**. Notice that not all the melody notes have been harmonised.

This version with block and broken chords ends in a **perfect cadence**.

A look back

Match each chord with its family member.

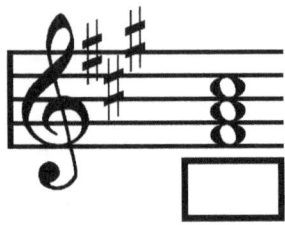

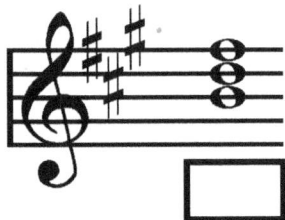

V^{7}b

IVc

Ic

II

III

IVc

Vb

V^{7}b

VI

Chord I -   Tonic

Chord II -   Supertonic

Chord III - Mediant

Chord IV -   Subdominant

Chord V -   Dominant

Chord V^7 - Dominant 7th

Chord VI -   Submediant

Family visitors

In each musical family _____ chord IV has a Cousin who can sometimes take

her place. Cousin is chord ____ or the supertonic. Father chord ____ can be replaced by

_____ chord ____, also known as the _____. Mother chord ____

can be substituted by _____ chord ____, also known as the _____.

Family relations

Each Major Family has a Relative Minor Family with the same key signature.

You can discover the Relative Minor Family by counting down on the keyboard ____

semitones from the root note of Mother's _____ chord in the Major key.

For example, the relative of **C Major** is ____ Minor. ____ Minor is related to **F Major**

and **A Major** to ____ **Minor.**

Harmonising melodies

On the following pages there are three melodies for you to harmonise.

Remember ...

Helpful hints

1. Use chords in root position, first inversion (b) and second inversion (c).

2. Do **not** use chords II, III or VI to end a piece.

3. Play safe by going home to Mother. Use a perfect cadence and end on the tonic.

4. Double the root or fifth of a chord.

5. Chord II is often used in its first inversion.

6. Never double the third except in chord IIb.

7. Never double the seventh of a dominant chord.

8. Do **not** use chords **II, III** and **VI too often**. Although these Minor chords add variety, they could make harmonies in Major keys sound sad. You will learn about harmonies in Minor keys in Section 10.

When you are satisfied, write your harmonies in the book before you look at the versions on pages 77 to 79.

Tune 1

Harmonise my tune. Draw 2/3 notes in the treble and 1 note in the bass to celebrate my special day.

IVc   I_____   V_____   IV   V   Vb

I_____   I_____

Vc   II   IIIb   IVb   V⁷b   I

Tune 2

Tune 3

I_____   Vb__   I   I___   IV_____

I   IIIc_____   IVb   VI

IIb   IVc Vb   I   Ib   V   V⁷b   I

Happy Birthday to you

Happy birthday to you.
Happy birthday to you.
Happy birthday dear Grandpa.
Happy birthday to you.

Kum Bah Yah

Michael, Row the Boat Ashore

SECTION 9

More neighbours — the magic circle of keys continues to grow

The relatives — Cousin II, Grandfather III and Grandmother VI

Uncle arrives — chord VII

First and second inversion revisited

The Leading Note (7th) and the third inversion of the Dominant 7th

Meet the family

You have met the three inner family members.

The **Inner Family** Consists of

Mother the **Tonic Chord I**

Daughter the **Subdominant Chord IV**

Father the **Dominant Chord V**

Father can also add a 7th to his chord.
He is then the **Dominant 7th Chord V^7**

You have also met three relatives.

Cousin is the **Supertonic Chord II**

Grandfather is the **Mediant Chord III**

Grandmother is the **Submediant Chord VI**

81

More neighbours

You will now meet some more Major families with their **Relative Minors**.

E Major with 4 sharps: F, C, G & D
and its Relative Minor **C♯ Minor**

A♭ Major with 4 flats: B, E, A & D
and its Relative Minor **F Minor**

The **Magic Circle of Keys** has grown.

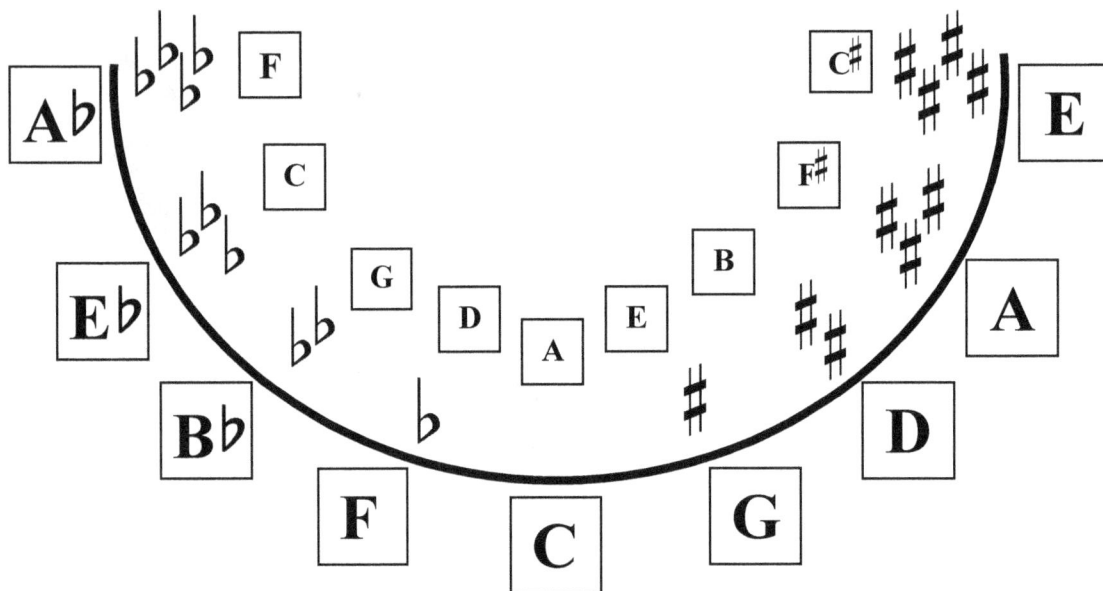

The complete **Circle of Keys** is on page 133.

Draw *with* key signatures:

Daughter's chord IV
in the **E Major** Family

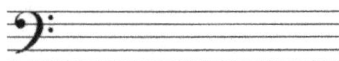

Mother's chord I
in the **A♭ Major** Family

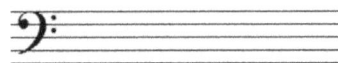

Father's chord V
in the **A♭ Major** Family

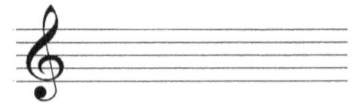

Chord I
in the **E Major** Family

Chord IV
in the **A♭ Major** Family

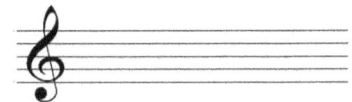

Dominant 7th chord

Here are **dominant** and **dominant 7th** chords of **E Major** in root position.

$$V \qquad V^7$$

Draw **dominant** and **dominant 7th** chords of the following keys in the same way.

G Major

$$V \qquad V^7$$

B♭ Major

$$V \qquad V^7$$

D Major

$$V \qquad V^7$$

A♭ Major

$$V \qquad V^7$$

Play each pair of chords and listen to their different sounds.

Harmony with the inner family

Here are two tunes for you to play in your new keys. They use the three chords of the **Inner family** plus Father's **dominant 7th**.

Using the relatives

Chords **II**, **III** and **VI** are Minor chords. If you use them occasionally in a Major key they add variety to your harmonies. Do **not** use chord **II**, **III** or **VI** in the last cadence of a piece. Use members of the Inner Family for that 'final' feel.

Play these two chords in **A Major**.
Cousin's Chord II may sometimes be used
instead of Daughter's Chord IV.

II   IV

Grandfather's Chord III can sometimes
take the place of Father's Chord V. Draw
and play both chords in **B♭ Major**.

III   V

Grandmother's Chord VI can sometimes
be used in place of Mother's Chord I.
Draw and play both chords in **A♭ Major**.

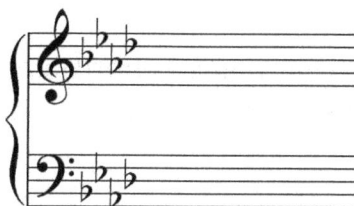

VI   I

Play these three pieces. Listen to the chords.

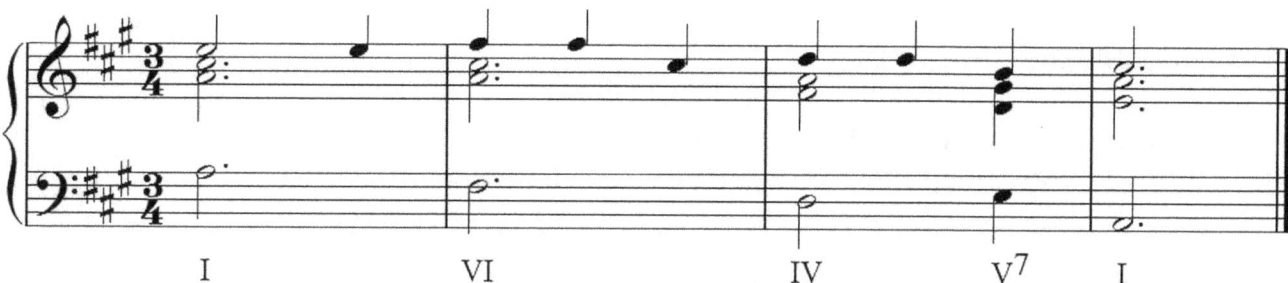

I   IV   V   I   II   V   V⁷   I

I   III   I   V   I   III   V⁷   I

I   VI   IV   V⁷   I

85

Chord VII

You have met every chord in the musical families except **Chord VII**.
Play all the **F Major** chords drawn below and listen to their sounds.

Chord VII (a diminished chord) is neither Major nor Minor, making it difficult to use. Think of it as an **Uncle** who very rarely visits.

Draw all the chords for **C Major**.

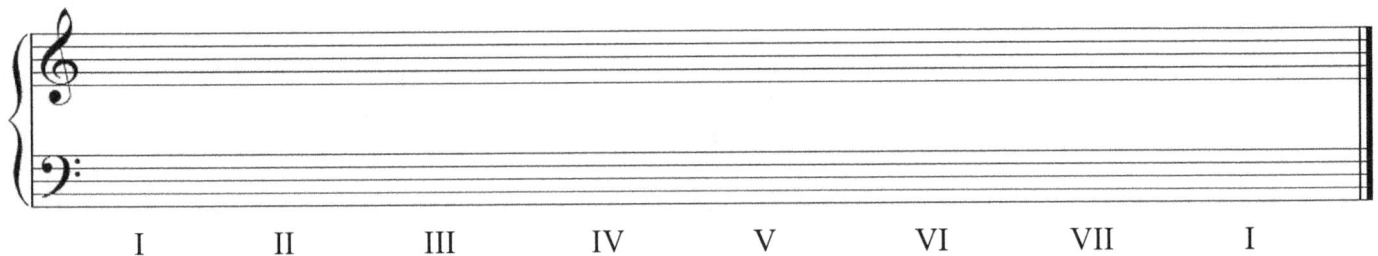

Play the chords and listen to their sounds.

The leading note

Although chord VII is difficult to use, the **7th note** of a scale is *very* useful. Known as the **Leading Note**, it *leads up* to the tonic.

Important Rules:

1. **Never** double the Leading Note.

2. If the **Dominant** Chord is followed by the **Tonic** Chord, the **Leading Note** must move **upwards** by **one semitone**.

Play the following examples:-

V   I

V   I

Now draw your own chords for **F Major** and **D** Major. Play and listen to your chords.

V   I

V   I

A quick look back

The E Major Family has __ sharps and its Relative Minor is __ Minor.

The A♭ Major Family has __ flats and its Relative Minor is __ Minor.

The Inner Family of chords.

chord I
tonic

chord __
dominant

chord __
subdominant

chord __
_____

Four Other Family Members.

chord __
supertonic

chord __
_____

chord __
_____

chord VII
formed on the
leading note

Sometimes Cousin (**II**) replaces Daughter (**IV**), Grandfather ( ) replaces Father ( ), and Grandmother ( ) replaces Mother ( ). Uncle chord ( ) is neither Major nor Minor.

The Leading Note of a scale is the __th note.

87

Chords In Major keys

Root position chords can be drawn on **any note** of the scale.

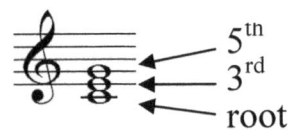

Play all these chords for two Major scales drawn in four different ways.

4 notes in the right hand

I   II   III   IV   V   VI   VII   I

4 notes in the left hand

I   II   III   IV   V   VI   VII   I

3 notes in the right hand and 1 in the left

2 notes in the right hand and 2 in the left

When **1st inversion chords** are formed on **every degree** of the scale, the **3rd** is now at the bottom. Play these 1st inversion chords in **B♭ Major**.

Ib   IIb   IIIb   IVb   Vb   VIb   VIIb   I

88

Draw and play all the first inversion chords for **D Major** in the *left hand only*.

Ib   IIb   IIIb   IVb   Vb   VIb   VIIb   Ib

Draw and play all the first inversion chords for **E Major** with *two notes in each clef*.
Remember to put the 3rd at the bottom.

Ib   IIb   IIIb   IVb   Vb   VIb   VIIb   Ib

Second inversion chords are mainly
formed on **Inner Family** notes.
Put the **5th** of the chord at the bottom.

Play these three second inversion chords in **A♭ Major**.

Ic IVc Vc

Complete and play these 2nd inversion chords of **E♭ Major**.

Ic IVc Vc

Play these **Inner Family triads** for **C Major** in root position, first and second inversions.

I   Ib   Ic   IV   IVb   IVc   V   Vb   Vc

89

Now play the same chords, this time shared between two hands. Try other Major keys.

I   Ib   Ic   IV   IVb   IVc   V   Vb   Vc

From the previous pages you saw that **chord V** can have only two inversions.

The **dominant 7th chord (V⁷)** has **three** possible **inversions** because of its extra note.

You build a third inversion in the same way as you build 1st and 2nd inversions and you distinguish a third inversion with the letter **d**.

F Major

V⁷   V⁷b   V⁷c   V⁷d

Some rules when using the *third inversion* of the dominant 7th:

1. Always put the 7th in the bass.

C major   G major   D major   A major   E major

add the missing bass notes

2. Do not double the 3rd or 7th notes.

C Major   F Major   B♭ Major   E♭ Major   A♭ Major

3. Double the root if you omit the 5th note.

C major   F major   G major   B♭ major   D major

4. Never omit the 7th note because the result would no longer be a V^7 chord.

Note that the 3rd inversion of Father's Dominant 7th Chord usually *resolves* to the first inversion of Mother's Tonic Chord, the 7th falling one step and the 3rd rising one step.

Play this melody in the key of **E♭ Major**.

Now play the harmonised melody. Put the **missing chord names** in the empty boxes.

I   IVc   I   V⁷d   ☐   IIIb

IV   Ib   ☐   I   ☐   V⁷b

VI   ☐   Ic   V   ☐   I

Check your answers.

Ib V IVc IV V⁷ (answers printed inverted)

92

Chords in Major keys

Match each chord with its family member.

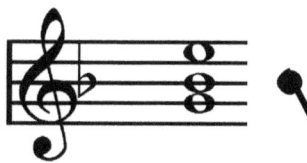
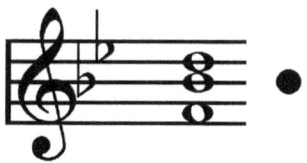
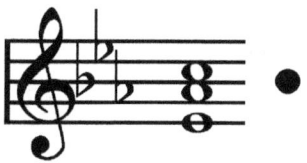

Ic

II

IIIb

IVc

Vc

V⁷d

VI

VIIb

SECTION 10

Harmonic and melodic Minor scales

Chords in Minor keys

Doubling the third

Binding, essential, passing and auxiliary notes

Modulation

Harmonic Minor scales

Play this harmonic Minor scale and notice that the **7th** note has been raised by one semitone ascending *and* descending.

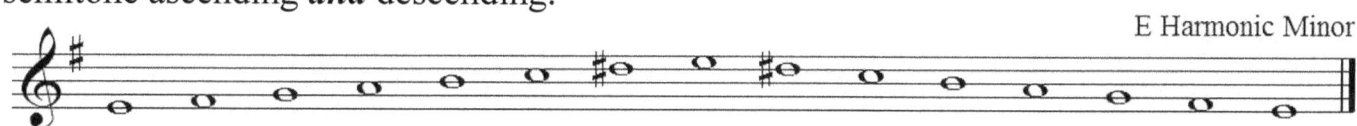

E Harmonic Minor

Over to you

Write the scale of **D Harmonic Minor** ascending and descending with key signature. Remember to raise the 7th note.

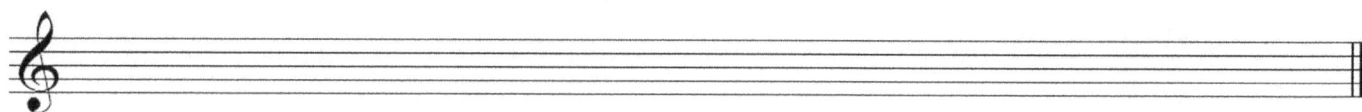

Now write the key signature and scale of **G Harmonic Minor** ascending and descending.

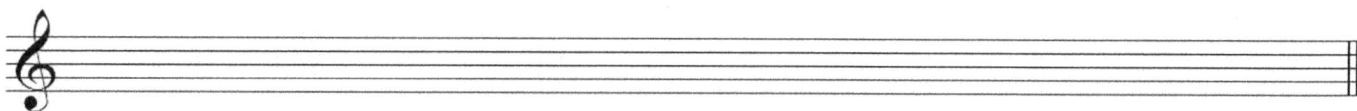

Play all the scales on this page. You will find other Minor Scales on pages 127 to 129.

Chords in Minor keys

Chords in Minor keys are usually formed on the notes of the **Harmonic Minor** scale. In **root position** you should build chords on notes **I, IV, V** and **VI**. *

Play these **D Minor** chords. Notice that the 7th note of the scale has been raised one semitone.

I   IV   V   VI

* Chords built on notes II, III and VII of Harmonic Minor.
Scales are scarcely ever used in harmony.

95

Now draw the chords in the key of E Minor.

I   IV   V   VI

In Minor Keys you can use six first inversion chords. The only *exception* is Grandfather's Mediant, chord III.

Add the **bottom note** to complete each of these first inversion chords in **A Minor**. Remember the raised 7th. Play and listen to all the chords.

Ib   IIb   IVb   Vb   V7b   VIb   VIIb

Second inversion chords in Minor Keys are mainly formed on the notes of the **Inner Family**.

Add the **top note** in the treble clef to complete these chords in **B Minor**. Play and listen to all the chords.

Ic   IVc   Vc

Answers

A minor: C, D, F, G#, A, B.
B minor: B, E, F#.

96

Here are melody notes in four different keys with a harmonised version below. Draw in the missing note for the chords marked ✳ to give two notes in each clef.

Play your chords and listen to the sounds.

Check your answers

Melodic Minor scales

A tune in a Minor key usually uses the **Melodic Minor Scale** in which you **raise** the 6th and 7th notes when **ascending** and **lower** them again when **descending**.

Here is the scale of **G Melodic Minor** in the treble and bass clefs. Play the scales with separate hands and then hands together.

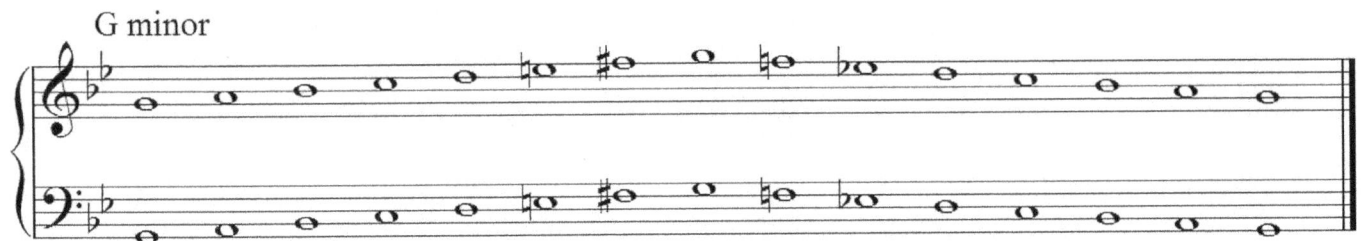

Write the scale of E Melodic Minor in both Treble and Bass clef. Play each scale with separate hands and hands together.

You will find all scales up to four sharps and four flats on pages 127 to 129.

Play this piece of music.

Is it written in **D Major** or **B Minor**?

Clues

D Major: its final melody note will probably be **D** with a bass note **D** and Mother's tonic chord **D**.

B Minor: it will probably end with Mother's tonic chord **B**. There may be **A♯**. There may also be **G♯** if the melodic form is used.

Play the following piece. Is it written in **G Major** or **E Minor**?

Using chords in Minor keys

Here are chords in the key of **G Minor**. Notice that there are two notes in the right hand and two in the left hand. Put the names of the chords in the empty boxes.

V [ ]   IVc [ ]   VII [ ]   [ ]   VIb [ ]   I

Here is a melody in G Minor. Add one ♩. to each named chord to complete the harmony with two notes in each clef. Play your harmonised melody.

I   IVb   Ic   VIb   VII   IVc   V   V⁷   I   I

Check your answers

Missing ♩. notes:
G, E♭, D, E♭, F♯, G, F♯, F♯, D, B♭

Ic   IVb   I   I   V⁷

99

Chords in Minor keys

Match each chord with its family member.

  **Ic**

 **IIb**

 **III**

 **IVc**

 **Vc**

 **V⁷b**

 **VI**

 **VIIb**

Doubling the third

If chord **VI** in a Minor key comes before or after chord **V** you may **double** the **3rd** instead of the root or 5th. Play these chords.

VI→V   V →VI

Add notes to complete the following chords, two notes in the right hand and two in the left.

I   I   I   Ib   IIb   IV   Vb   V^7 Vc   V^{7}d   IVb

Complete this harmonisation. Use the chord numbers to help you. Now play the piece.

I   IVb   Vb   I   IIb   IV

V^{7}d   Ib   V^7 I

Binding notes

When writing harmony, the aim is to move as smoothly as possible from note to note. Using a **binding note** helps us to do this. Look at this example in **E Major** where chords **I** and **V** are next to each other.

The binding note, **B**, is the same in all three chords. The other notes in the right hand move stepwise, first down then up.

Here is an example, with chords **I** and **IV**. This time **E** is the binding note. The other notes in the right hand move stepwise, first up then down. Play all the chords carefully.

Over to you

Complete the chords in the following four Major keys. Use a **binding note** to connect the three chords in each sequence.

Melodic decoration

1. *Essential notes*

We rarely harmonise every melody note with its own separate chord, except perhaps for hymns and stately tunes such as the National Anthem.

Melody notes that are harmonised but *not with their own separate chords* are called **essential notes**. Here is an example with the essential notes clearly shown.

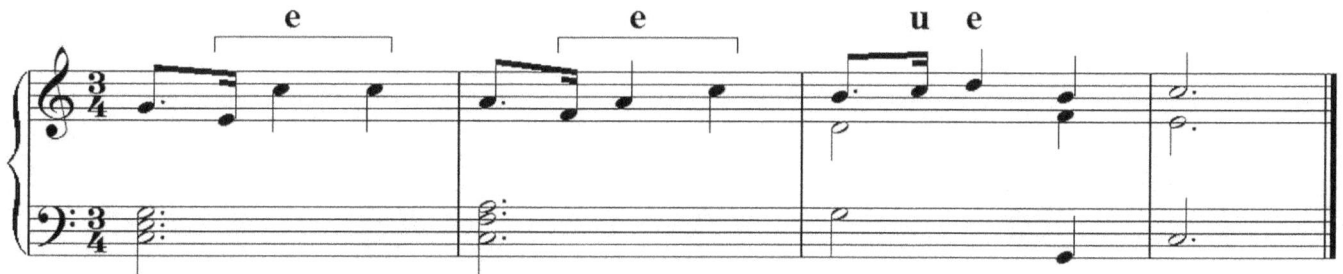

The note marked **u** is called an **unessential note** because it is *not* from the same chord.

2. *Passing notes*

These are **unessential** notes because they do not belong to the harmonised chords. Nevertheless **passing notes** add a great deal to the melodic decoration.

Passing notes move **step by step** either upwards or downwards. They form a smooth link between harmonised notes.

Play this example and notice the use of block chords. The **p** marks the passing notes.

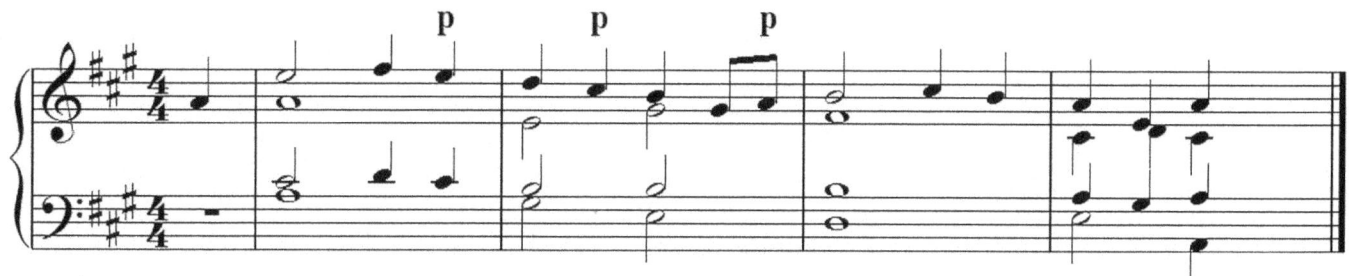

Now play this example and notice the use of broken chords. Mark the passing notes.

3. *Auxiliary notes*

These unessential notes add to the melodic decoration but unlike passing notes they move a step *above or below* a note of the harmony and then *return* to that note.

Play this example. The auxiliary notes have been marked **a**. Notice the use of three-note chords in the left hand. This is another style for you to try.

Mark the six auxiliary notes in this passage. Play it and listen to the variety of chords.

N.B. Ornaments are largely built from auxiliary notes. These can be studied in detail in Theory Is Fun Grade 4.

Over to you

Use this piece of music to practise melodic decoration with unessential notes. Add *one* **passing** note at places marked **p** and *one* **auxiliary** note at places marked **a**.

Play your enriched composition and listen to the effect of the notes you have added.

Modulation – change of key

This is changing key *during* a piece of music usually without a change in the key signature. Modulation occurs most easily with families living near each other on the magic circle, i.e. Major and Relative Minor or keys with one sharp or flat more or less than the *home* key.

For example:

G Major can most easily modulate to the keys of E Minor, D Major, B Minor, C Major and A Minor.

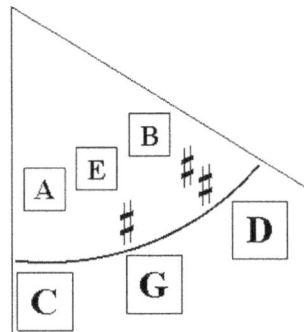

G Minor can most easily modulate to the keys of B♭ Major, C Minor, E♭ Major, D Minor and F Major.

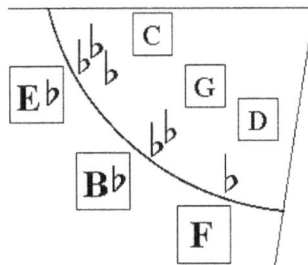

The full magic circle is on page 133.

Complete the following two examples.

home key	*most easily modulates to keys of*
E♭ Major	_____ _____ _____ _____ _____
F♯ Minor	_____ _____ _____ _____ _____

Over to you

The following piece modulates from a Major key to its relative Minor. The leading note in the new key rises to its tonic to establish the new key.

Decide for yourself

Play this piece. It begins in the key of _____. In bars 8 to 9, the music modulates

from _____ to _____. The piece ends in the key of _____.

SECTION 11

Helpful relatives

Chart to use for adding notes to chords

Experimenting with rhythm

We'll use a mixture of root, 1st, 2nd and 3rd inversion chords.

We won't harmonise every note or use the 2nd inversion too often.

6 Pieces to harmonise and play

Helpful relatives

1. Father's **dominant chord V^7b**

This chord is used for a *strong* perfect cadence in a Major or Minor key because it has **two** notes pulling to resolve.

Play these three resolutions. Complete the last one yourself.

C major   E minor   D major

V^7b I V^7b I V^7b I

Now play this passage and notice how chord V^7b provides a perfectly natural link as you modulate from D Major to E Minor.

2. Cousin's **supertonic chord II**

Try chord II especially if you are modulating to a *flatter* key.
Example: modulation from **C Major** to **F Major** using the **D Minor chord II** as a link. Play all the chords.

C Major   F Major

I   II   VI V^7b I

Notice how my chord II in one key becomes chord VI in the new key

109

3. Grandmother's **submediant chord VI**

Try chord VI especially if you are modulating to a *sharper* key.

Example: modulation from **C Major** to **G Major** using the **A Minor chord VI** as a link. Play all the chords.

C Major   G Major
I   VI | II   V   I

Notice how my chord VI in one key becomes chord II in the new key

Adding notes to chords

Extra notes can enrich the sound of chords. You already know how to draw chord V^7 by adding a seventh to the dominant chord. Now you can enrich other chords with extra notes by adding sixths, sevenths and ninths.

Add to chord	I	II	III	IV	V	VII
● sixth	●			●		
● seventh	●	●	●			●
● ninth	●				●	

Play and listen carefully to the following examples. Complete the names of the chords in the empty boxes underneath them.

Chords based on the C major scale with their root in the bass clef

I   [   ]   IV⁶   [   ]   II⁷   [   ]   [   ]   [   ]

110

Over to you

Play this piece and listen to the chords enriched with a sixth, seventh or ninth note.

Changing notes in chords

The triad **C-F-G** is the 'suspended fourth' chord that likes to resolve to the **C Major** tonic chord **C-E-G**. The triad **G-B-D♯** is an 'augmented fifth' chord.

Play and listen to the following chords.

Have fun changing notes in other chords.

A quick recap

Describe each of the following tonic notes as **auxiliary**, **binding**, **essential** or **passing**.

1. _____   2. _____

3. _____   4. _____

111

Modulation is changing ___ *during* a piece usually without a change in ___ _____.

Modulation occurs most easily with families near to each other on the magic circle, i.e. **m**_____ and **r**_____ **m**_____ keys *or* keys with one sharp or one flat more or less than the **h**_____ key.

Father's **chord** ___ is a very useful link between two keys. Cousin's **chord II** is useful when modulating to a _____ key. Grandmother's **chord VI** is useful when modulating to a _____ key. Chords can be enriched by adding 6ths, _____ and _____ or by changing notes.

Experimenting with rhythm

On the following pages there are some new rhythms for you to enjoy with three harmonised pieces to play and three melodies for you to harmonise and play.

Remember

1. Father's dominant 7th can resolve onto Mother's tonic chord and Daughter's subdominant chord can lead to Father's chord V or Mother's chord I.

2. Cousin's chord II may replace Daughter's chord IV, Grandfather's chord III may replace Father's chord V and Grandmother's Chord VI may replace Mother's Chord I.

3. Do not use chords II, III or VI too often and do not use them in a final cadence. Try to make use of the 1st inversion of Cousin's chord II and 2nd inversions of Mother, Father and Daughter chords.

4. Double the root or fifth of a chord but only double the third in Chord IIb. Never double the leading note or the seventh note of a dominant chord.

5. To end a piece use a perfect cadence with Father's chord V or V^7 going home to Mother's tonic chord. If the tonic chord follows the dominant chord, the leading note moves upwards by one semitone.

Oom-pah rhythm

Play, sing and enjoy this piece.

Notice the steady rhythm of the left-hand.

113

Oom-pah-pah rhythm

Keep an oom-pah-pah beat in the left- hand.

Complete the harmonisation of this melody. Play and sing it.

114

Swinging blues

Twinkle, twinkle little star,
I don't wonder what you are.
Just a ball of white hot gases,
Cooling down to molten masses.

Here is a new rhythm for a well-known tune. Notice the simplicity of the notes in the left-hand as you play this version.

115

Syncopation

This well-known carol has
been given a syncopated
rhythm. Keep the left-hand
simple when you harmonise this tune.

Good King Wen - ces - las look'd out On the feast of Ste - phen,

When the snow lay round a - bout, Deep and crisp and ev - en.

Bright - ly shone the moon that night, Though the frost was cru - el,

When a poor man came in sight Gath - 'ring win - ter fu - el.

Off-beat rhythm

Play this piece. Note that the left-hand has the chords and the right-hand single notes.

Music does not have to be complicated to be effective. Rhythm is so important.

Over to you

Harmonise this tune in an **offbeat** style.

Use three- and four-note chords in the bass clef. Their numbers are given to help you.

SECTION 12

Music from Upbeat! For Piano by Alison Hounsome

Melody notes of 3 pieces for you to harmonise

Full scores for you to play and compare with your versions

Lotus Blossom Lullaby

Alison Hounsome

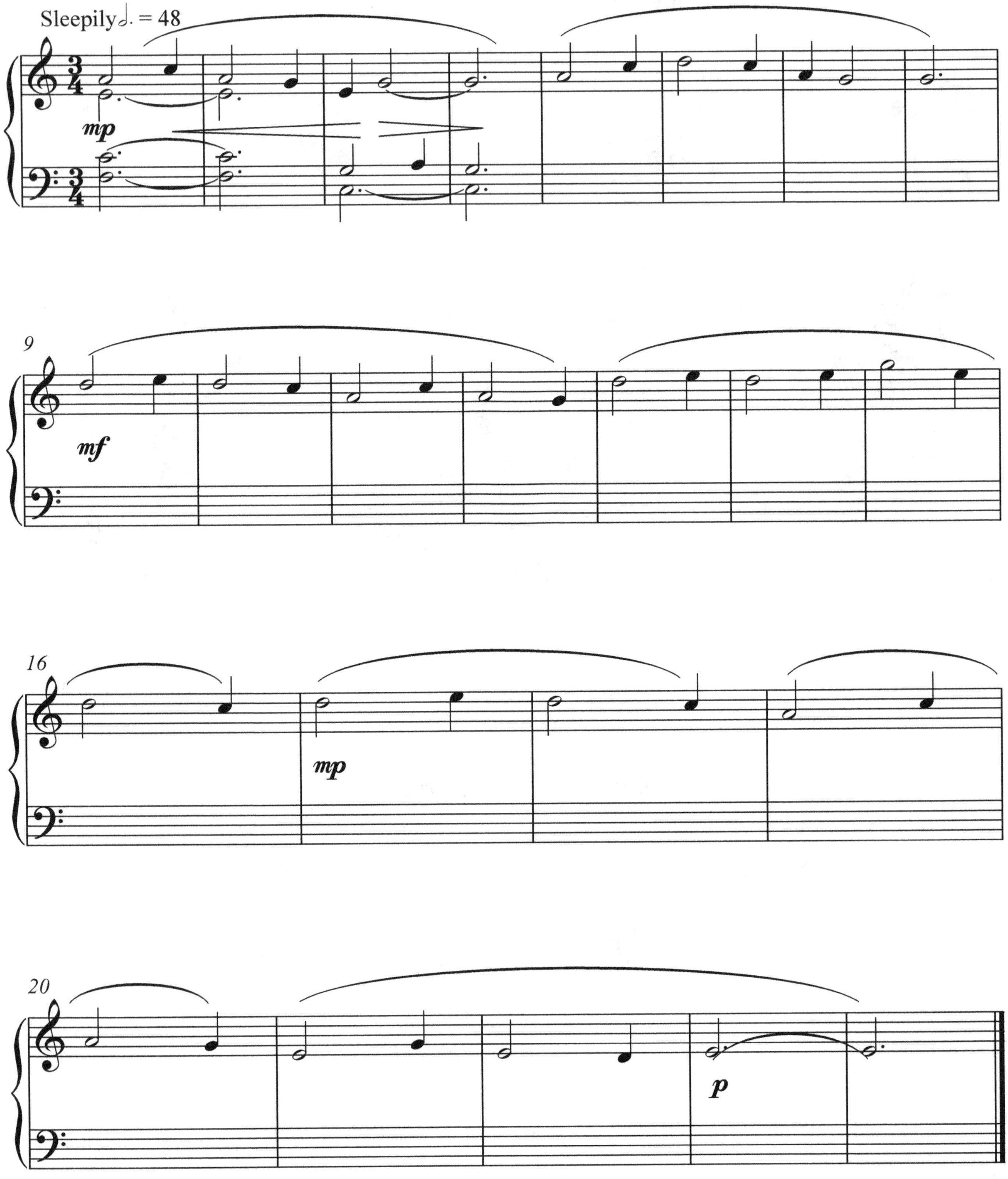

Easy Trapezy

Feel one-in-a-bar ♩. = 56

Alison Hounsome

Caribbean Cocktail

Bright Calypso style ♩ = 116

Alison Hounsome

Lotus Blossom Lullaby

Alison Hounsome

Easy Trapezey

Alison Hounsome

Feel one-in-a-bar ♩. = 56

Caribbean Cocktail

Bright Calypso style ♩ = 116

Alison Hounsome

con ped.

SECTION 13

REFERENCE LIBRARY
QUIET PLEASE

Major scales and their relative minors

Melodic minor scales

Fingering chord sequences

Useful chord progressions

The magic circle of keys

List of terms

Major scales and their relative minors

Remember in harmonic minor scales to raise
the seventh note ascending *and* descending.

C Major

A Minor

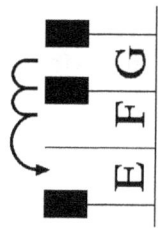

G Major

E Minor

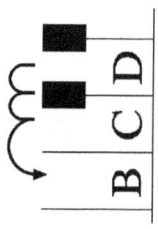

D Major

B Minor

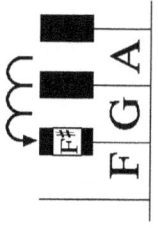

A Major

F♯ Minor

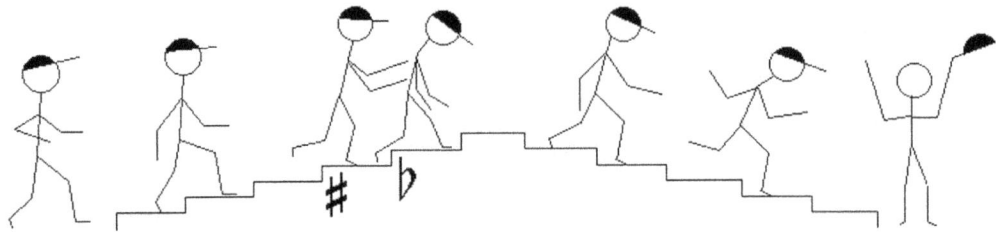

E Major

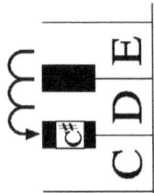

C♯ Minor

F Major

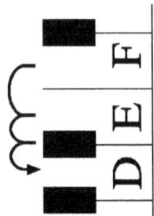

D Minor

B♭ Major

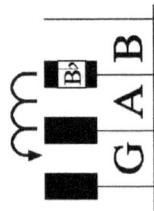

G Minor

E♭ Major

C Minor

A♭ Major

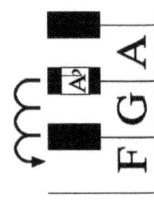

F Minor

Melodic minor scales

Remember in a melodic minor scale to raise the 6th and 7th notes ascending and to lower them again when descending.

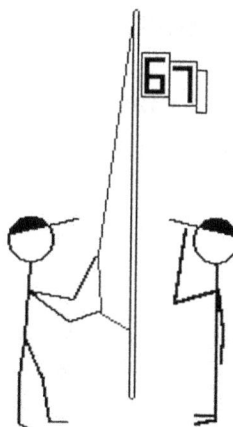

Fingering chord sequences

Some chords are easier to play than others. Here are some useful chord sequences that are fairly easy to finger and play.

I   IV   V   I

chord I

C   E   G   C

chord IV

F   F   A   C

chord V

G   D   G   B

chord I

C   E   G   C

130

Useful chord progressions

Consistent fingering makes playing easier. Try the following fingering and chord sequences in other major and minor keys.

One note in the left hand

Two notes in the left hand

The 7th note of chord V7 as an essential note.

The 7th note of chord V7 as a passing note.

Practise harmonising scales in different keys. Try using enriched chords (see page 110).

Finger and play the following examples.

132

The magic circle of keys

The **Major** families on the **outside** of the circle have the same key signature as their **Minor** relatives on the **inside** of the circle.

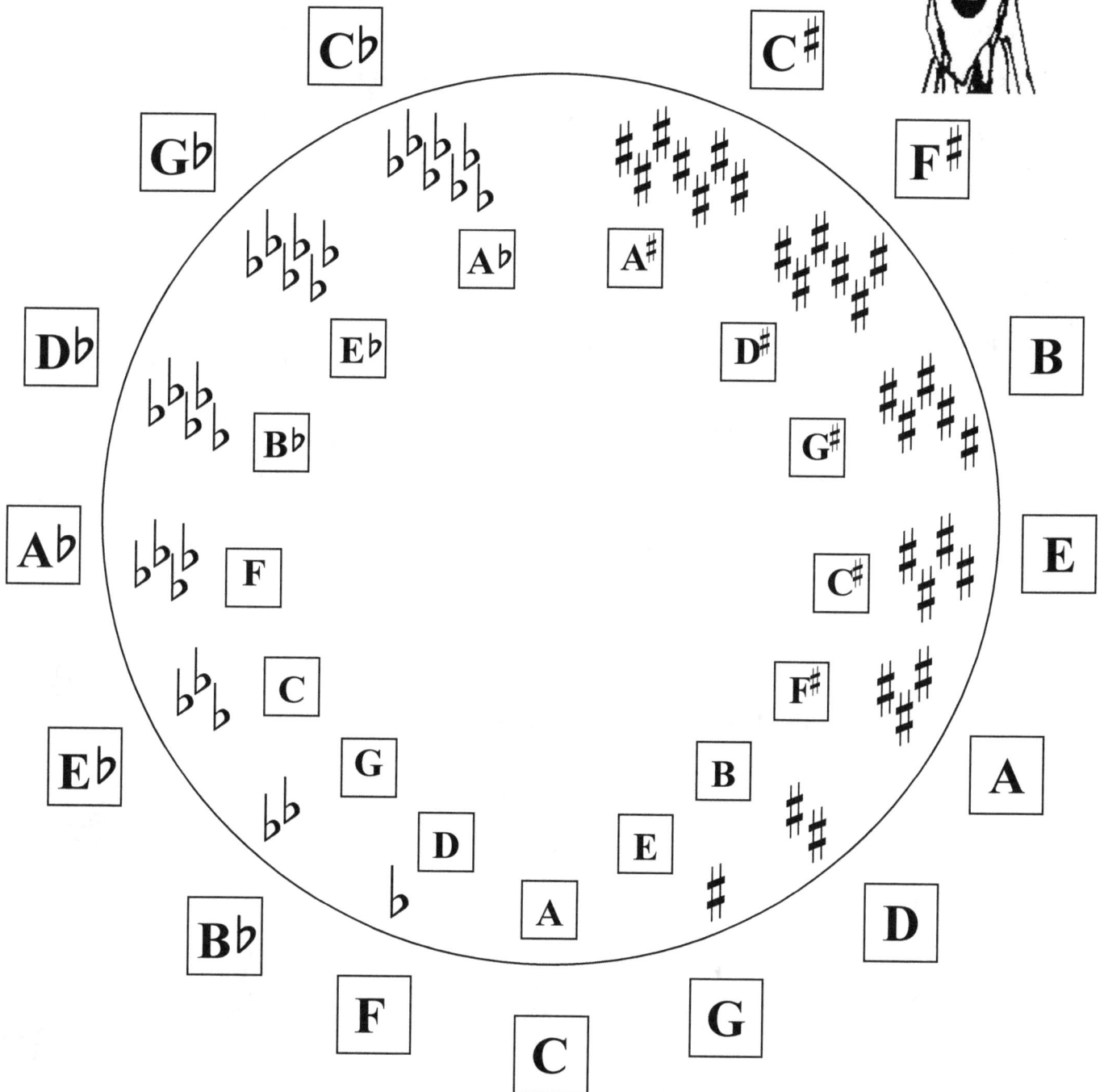

133

List of terms

auxiliary note   unessential notes in a chord sequence that move by step, up or down, then back again

binding note   a note common to two or more consecutive chords

broken chord   the notes of a chord played one after the other

cadence   the half or full close of a musical phrase or section

    imperfect   chord I or IV going to chord V suggesting a pause for breath

    perfect   chord V going to chord I with a strong feeling of ending

    plagal   chord IV going to chord I with a weaker feeling of ending

chord   two or more notes that are played together

chord in close position   the notes of a chord are as close together as possible

chord in open position   the notes of a chord are spread widely

chord I (or Ia)   tonic chord in root position

    Ib   tonic chord in first inversion

    Ic   tonic chord in second inversion

    a   letter to show root position

    b   letter to show first inversion

    c   letter to show second inversion

    d   letter to show third inversion

    II   supertonic chord

    III   mediant chord

    IV   subdominant chord

    V   dominant chord

    V^7   dominant 7th chord

    V^{7}b   dominant 7th chord in its first inversion

    VI   submediant chord

    VII   chord formed on the leading note

dominant	5th note of a scale and the chord grown from that note:
[Father]	e.g. G and G-B-D in the scale of C Major
dominant 7th	dominant chord with an added 7th note: e.g. G-B-D-F in the C Major scale
doubling	the same note (root or 5th and, in a minor key, perhaps 3rd in chord II) used twice in the same chord
essential notes	notes from the same chord that are not separately harmonised
first inversion	chord with its 3rd note at the bottom
leading note **[Uncle]**	7th note of a scale and the chord grown from that note: e.g. G and G-B♭-D♭ in the A♭ Major scale
mediant **[Grandfather]**	3rd note of a scale and the chord grown from that note: e.g. F♯ and F♯-A-C♯ in the scale of D Major
modulation	changing key during a piece without a change in the key signature
passing notes	unessential notes in a chord sequence that move by steps *either* up *or* down
resolving	movement of a note or chord to a more satisfying note or chord: e.g. chord V^7 to chord I
root	note from which a chord grows: e.g. C is the root of the tonic chord of C Major
root position	the root of a chord is at the bottom or in the bass
second inversion	chord with its 5th note at the bottom
subdominant **[Daughter]**	4th note of a scale and the chord grown from that note: e.g. B♭ and B♭-D-F in the F Major scale
submediant **[Grandmother]**	6th note of a scale and the chord grown from that note: e.g. F♯ and F♯-A-C♯ in the A Major scale
supertonic **[Cousin]**	2nd note of a scale and the chord grown from that note: e.g. C and C-E♭-G in the B♭ Major scale
triad	a three-note chord: e.g. the tonic triad G-B-D of the G Major scale
tonic **[Mother]**	1st note of a scale and the chord grown from that note: e.g. E♭ and E♭-G-B♭ in the E♭ Major scale

Also by Maureen Cox

Theory is Fun Grade 1   paperback
ISBN 0 9516940 8 1

Treble clef, bass clef, notes and letter names. Time names and values. Dotted notes, tied notes and rests. Accidentals, tones and semitones. Key signatures and scales (C, G, D & F major). Degrees of the scale, intervals and tonic triads. Time signatures and bar-lines. Writing music and answering rhythms. Musical terms dictionary and list of signs.

Theory is Fun Grade 2   paperback
ISBN 1 898771 02 2

Major (A, Bb & Eb) and minor (A, E & D) key signatures and scales Degrees of the scale and intervals. Tonic triads. Piano keyboard, tones and semitones. Time signatures. Grouping notes and rests, triplets. Two ledger lines below and above the staves. Writing four-bar rhythms. More musical terms and signs.

Theory is Fun Grade 3   paperback
ISBN 1 898771 00 6

Major & minor key signatures 4 sharps or flats. Harmonic and melodic minor scales. Degrees of the scale, intervals, tonic triads. Simple and compound time signatures. Grouping notes & rests. Transposition at the octave. More than two ledger lines. Writing four-bar rhythms, anacrusis. Phrases and more musical terms & signs.

Theory is Fun Grade 4   paperback
ISBN 1 898771 01 4

All key signatures to 5 sharps or flats. Alto clef. Chromatic scale, double sharps & flats. Technical names of notes in the diatonic scale. Simple & compound time, duple, triple, quadruple. Primary triads, tonic, subdominant & dominant. All diatonic intervals up to an octave. Recognising ornaments. Four-bar rhythms and rhythms to words. Families of orchestral instruments and their clefs. More musical terms, including French

Theory is Fun Grade 5   paperback
ISBN 0 9516940 9 X

All key signatures to 7 sharps or flats. Tenor clef and scales. Compound intervals: major, minor, perfect, diminished and augmented. Irregular time signatures, quintuple & septuple. Tonic, supertonic, subdominant & dominant chords. Writing at concert pitch. Short & open score. Orchestral instruments in detail. Composing a melody for instrument or voice. Perfect, imperfect & plagal cadences. More musical terms, including German

Theory is Fun Grades 1 - 5 in a Nutshell   paperback
ISBN 1 898771 17 0

Major, relative harmonic & melodic minor keys. Chromatic scales. Regular & irregular time signatures. Beaming & grouping of notes & rests. Intervals, chords and cadences. Instruments of the orchestra. Concert pitch & transposition. Short & open score. Composing a melody for instrument or voice. Musical terms and signs.

Theory is Fun Activity Book 1   paperback
ISBN 1 898771 12 X

Letter names and notes in treble and bass clef. Time names and note values. Dotted notes and rests. Key signatures and time signatures. Degrees of the scale and intervals. Musical terms and signs. Introduction to aural practice.

Theory is Fun in a Nutshell   Kindle electronic book
ISBN 978 0 9866549 0 9

Major, relative harmonic & melodic minor keys. Chromatic scales. Regular & irregular time signatures. Beaming & grouping of notes & rests. Intervals, chords and cadences. Instruments of the orchestra. Concert pitch & transposition. Short & open score. Composing a melody for instrument or voice. Musical terms and signs.

Musical Terms & Signs in a Nutshell

ISBN 978 0 9866549 7 8   Kindle electronic book
ISBN 978 1 9879260 8 8   paperback

A dictionary and a handy chart of all the major and minor key signatures.

Musical Terms Word Search In A Nutshell   paperback
ISBN 9780986654992

160 Italian, 20 French and 20 German Musical Terms; 20 graduated word searches with hidden musical terms to be found and then written in their original language; 20 answer grids with written English meanings required; alphabetical list of 40 terms after each section; 6 tests to match words and meanings; answers to all six tests

Books of Music	Composer	ISBN
Upbeat for Piano - Level 0	Alison Bowditch (*)	1 898771 09 X
Upbeat for Piano - Level 1	Alison Bowditch	1 898771 04 9
Upbeat for Piano - Level 2	Alison Bowditch	1 898771 05 7
Upbeat for Piano - Level 3	Alison Bowditch	1 898771 06 5
Upbeat for Piano - Level 4	Alison Bowditch	1 898771 07 3
Upbeat for Piano - Level 5	Alison Bowditch	1 898771 08 1
Upbeat! For Clarinet Book 1	Alison Bowditch	1 898771 18 9
Upbeat! For Flute or Oboe Book 1	Alison Bowditch	1 898771 19 7
Upbeat! For Saxophone Book 1	Alison Bowditch	1 898771 22 7
Upbeat! For Violin Book 1	Roy Robinson	1 898771 20 0
Upbeat! For Violin Book 2	Roy Robinson	1 898771 21 9
Upbeat for Small Jazz Groups	Roy Robinson	1 898771 15 4

Books and music available from Music Exchange (Manchester) Ltd www.music-exchange.co.uk. Electronic books available from www.amazon.com and www.amazon.co.uk

(*) Alison Bowditch now known as Alison Hounsome

Also by Maureen Cox

Blast Off with Music Theory Book 1   paperback
ISBN 1 56939 084 3

Treble clef and bass clef note names. Basic note values, including dotted notes, tied notes and rests. Accidentals, half and whole steps. Key signatures and major scales. Degrees of the scale, intervals and tonic triads. Basic time signatures. Basic rules of music writing. Music dictionary and list of signs.

Blast Off with Music Theory Book 2   paperback
ISBN 1 56939 085 1

Key signatures and major scales through 3 sharps and flats. Key signatures and minor scales through 1 sharp and flat. More about melodic and harmonic intervals. Sixteenth notes and rests, triplets. Tonic triads through 3 sharps and flats. Time signatures of 2/2 and 3/8. Grouping of notes when writing. More about ledger line notes. Music dictionary and list of signs.

Blast Off with Music Theory Book 3   paperback
ISBN 1 56939 086 X

Key signatures and major scales through 4 sharps and flats. Key signatures and minor scales through 2 sharps and 4 flats. Major and minor tonic triads. Simple and compound time signatures. Transposition. Note values, including dotted eighth notes. More ledger lines. Writing four-measure rhythms. The phrase. Music dictionary and list of signs.

Blast Off with Music Theory Book 4   paperback
ISBN 1 56939 087 8

Major and minor key signatures. Minor scales. Double sharps and flats. Scale degree names. Chromatic scales. Transposition by 2nds and 3rds. Simple & compound time signatures. Duplets and triplets. Thirty-second notes. Primary triads and inversions. Augmented and diminished intervals. Augmented and diminished triads. Common melodic ornaments. Music dictionary and music signs.

Blast Off with Music Theory Book 5   paperback
ISBN 1 56939 088 6

Major and minor key signatures. Circle of fifths. Major and minor scales. Pentatonic and whole-tone scales. Alto and tenor clefs. Instruments of the orchestra. Sixty-fourth notes and double-dotted note values. Irregular rhythmic figures. Irregular time signatures. Plagal, authentic and half cadences. Writing using music shorthand.

Blast Off books available in North America from F J H Music Company Inc www.fjhmusic.com

www.ingramcontent.com/pod-product-compliance
Lightning Source LLC
Chambersburg PA
CBHW080935040426
42443CB00015B/3421